VIBRATE
HIGHER
DAILY

LALAH DELIA

HarperOne
An Imprint of HarperCollins*Publishers*

VIBRATE HIGHER DAILY

LIVE YOUR POWER

Library of Congress Cataloging-in-Publication Data
Names: Delia, Lalah, 1974- author.
Title: Vibrate higher daily : live your power / Lalah Delia.
Description: First edition. | New York, NY : HarperOne, [2019]
Identifiers: LCCN 2019015465| ISBN 9780062905147 (hardcover) |
ISBN 9780062905123 (trade pb)
Subjects: LCSH: Energy medicine. | Vibration—Therapeutic use. | Healing |
Spiritual life.
Classification: LCC RZ421 .D45 2019 | DDC 615.8/52—dc23
LC record available at https://lccn.loc.gov/2019015465

20 21 22 23   TC   10 9 8 7 6 5

To my children, India and Ahsiah.
As you've grown, I've grown.
As I've grown, you've grown.
We've grown into the closest of spiritual friends.

Thanks for thinking I'm a "cool parent."

Sweet Mother, gracious you,
for hugging me, feeding me, and putting on Latin
music every time I came over.
I never fully understood your journey, until I had to heal
from my own.
Now I understand where your power, compassion,
and grace come from.

Thanks for the transfigurable journey that
has been ours.
All said and done, I bow to you.

Thank you also, Mother, for the special homemade
chocolate-covered strawberries every holiday.
I miss them. And haven't had the interest yet to
try anyone else's.

I've sent love to you daily. Confident you've received it,
because of the many beautiful ways you've
sent your love back.

Beloved Father, you've been one of my
greatest teachers.
Thanks for still loving me and not un-fathering me or
saying "peace I'm out" during the toughest times.
Thanks for sticking in there, Dad!

You and Mother are alchemists.

And to you.
Thank you for allowing this book to be with you
at this now-moment,
and in future moments to come.

~ May vibrating higher daily see you through. ~

CONTENTS

1   ANOTHER WAY OF BEING | 1

2   SELF | 43

3   OTHERS | 111

4   VIBRATING HIGHER IN THE WORLD | 155

    A LETTER OF LOVE: EPILOGUE | 215

    ACKNOWLEDGMENTS | 219

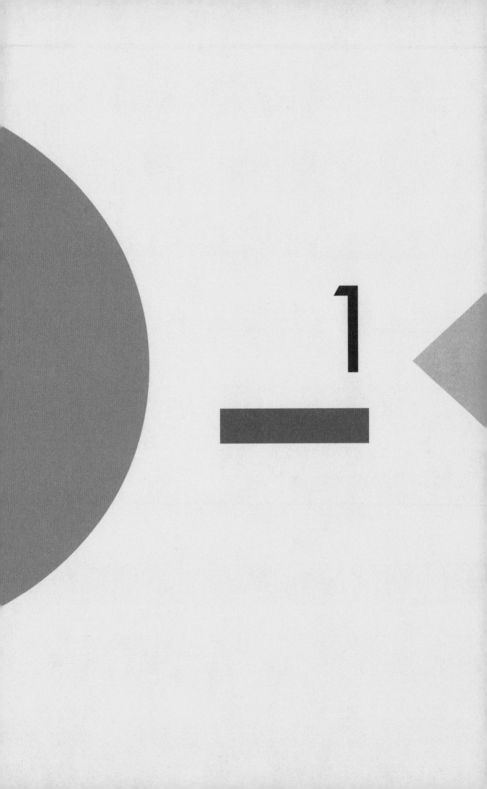

1

She remembered
who she was, and
the game changed.

ANOTHER WAY OF BEING

How do you thrive in a world that does not honor who and what you are—at the most real level? And how is it okay that we have come to this?

In a world that is ever evolving, expanding, and creating newer and more advanced versions of just about everything, we are still unfulfilled as a species. We are still longing. We are still warring. We are still not at peace. And we are still searching for the meaning of life, for the key to a better life, and for higher purpose.

Until we live from a place of connection to who and what we are—and what all things around us are—we are living out of harmony and beneath our inherent higher potential. A world living beneath its potential is what we have allowed planet Earth to become, hence, why we see so much chaos, imbalance, and dis-ease. The good news is, there is another way of being in the world. There is a better way to exist, rise, move beyond, and take our power back.

There is a deeper part of each of us beyond our race, ethnicity, gender, class, and appearance—a vital part. This is our vibration: a whole-body energy, always vibrating in response to the communicative connections between the mind, body, spirit, and all things. No matter where you're from, what your social class, or the color of your skin, vibration is vibration. We all feel it. And we're all affected by it in the same way. It's a universal thing. Everybody feels the effect of vibrations, and everyone is vibration.

There's a pathway of higher potential and power that, when honored, transforms your reality—and you. When it becomes the way you relate to all things in life, you are empowered. So instead of living a life of inducing, or being continually affected by, stress and negativity, I invite you to enter a life that reduces, overcomes, and transcends it.

This book is here to encourage and support you while challenging you to expand your way of thinking, living, and being. In essence, it's a sacred disruption, to the programming and consciousness you may have been living life from, up to now, retrospectively-speaking.

If you are outgrowing

who you've been,

you are right on

schedule.

Keep evolving.

MY
STORY

Today, I no longer live in the consciousness that I used to; one where I identified as a victim who is stuck, powerless, and purposeless. The process I share in this book led to the reconfiguration of my entire life, my physical health, even reconfiguring my appearance.

As I reflect on my journey and the experiences I've had with trauma, despair, domestic violence, emotional pain, heartbreak, a limited mindset, toxic relationships, and the sticky places I've been in and out of, I send myself love, not judgment. I do so because, at the time of those experiences, I didn't know about vibration. It was there all along, as it is in us all, but I wasn't at a place where I could yet recognize it within myself. I was living and experiencing life through a lower vibration and a limited mindset. And as with vibrations, came the life experiences to match.

When I was a young girl, I lived in the heart of South Central Los Angeles's "war zone" neighborhood—South Central as we called it. In our community, gang life, liquor stores, hustlers, broken dreams, flashy street styles, and beautiful people with unrealized higher potential existed on every street corner and stared back at you in passing. On a vibrational level, much was low, from the food quality to the education quality to the lack of wellness and self-development resources. The culture of lack within inner cities such as where I grew up has a direct adverse effect on the cultural tone and overall quality of life for masses of people and their personal and shared experiences. South Central Los Angeles in the 1980s and 1990s was a new kind of struggle and negative vortex for pretty much everyone there. And, so much was contributing to it. It was a time when crime was at an all-time high. A world where we were fed low vibrations, masked as the norm, and where the culture was, as I came to realize, being underserved vibrationally. And as with most urban communities still, it was common for us youth growing up in that environment to create peer bonds through our pain. We were all seeking affirmation and validation of some kind from one another.

I am grateful, through it all, that I had an advocate. I spent most of my childhood with my father, a man who was many things: an entrepreneur full of dreams, a transplant from New Mexico, and a practicing Buddhist, here and there. My father's ability to keep a positive mindset and his "pursuit of happiness" while in the midst of such an environment as South Central had a deep foundational impact on me. No matter what went on in the war zone neighborhood surrounding us, my father always created good vibrations and a positive atmosphere in our home. He had a way of energetically turning our home into a sanctuary and a safe haven.

My strongest memories about our home environment are of

dancing in front of the television to *Soul Train* on beautiful Saturday afternoons, hearing lots of '70s and '80s soul records playing, laughing, the burning of incense, and feeling pure love. He knew how to turn up the vibes in this way and shift our atmosphere into something higher, lighter, and better for the soul. And sure enough, to this day, dancing around at home, music, laughter, incense, and love are some of the essential go-to medicines for my soul. Powerfully, they bring me back to myself, every time.

My father did the best he could with what we had to work with. Using his Buddhist mindset and his joy for life, he taught me the skills for navigating our surroundings, and its potential traps. With a deep inner peace, a compassionate mindset, and a passion for progress, he instilled in me how to rise above our environment and the ability to see our situation and time there as temporary. Yet in spite of his most necessary, intentional, and urgent efforts to shelter me, including eventually moving out of South Central, I was, on many levels, still affected by the negative elements around us. The various effects felt close to unavoidable.

What I didn't yet know was how to respond to high and low vibrations in my environment. At times, I'd find myself swaying, adapting, and conforming to both energies. Many of us feel this tension. We are all empathic to some degree, and not knowing how to listen to our inner power when outside forces are strong creates imbalance and strains our progress.

Our past is a force that
doesn't always like to
see its end come.
And our future is a force
that doesn't want us
to abort it.

Competing Worlds

Now, on one of my shoulders was my father, shaping me for a higher potential life, beyond our environment at the time of '80s and '90s inner-city street culture. On the other shoulder was a collection of traumas. My initiation into the writing and work I do today was—like it is for so many others—through the path of pain and suffering.

Even though my parents did the best they knew how to protect me, deep pain had entered my life in four main ways. Over a short period of time, I was sexually violated as a child by a trusted teenage caretaker. At the same time, my parents had divorced, and I was not adapting well to it. I slipped into a state of depression, so much so that at the age of nine, I told my mother that I wanted to die because my family was broken. On top of all of this, at the age of five I had been diagnosed with a form of epilepsy known as petit mal. Every time I came out of a seizure at school, I'd "come back to" a crowd of laughing children, many of whom mocked and bullied me without fail. This painfully humiliating time happened all throughout lower grade school, until I eventually (and gratefully) outgrew the seizures at the age of twelve. And a very welcomed healing it was.

In addition to these early childhood traumas, I also experienced verbal abuse from my mother's fourth husband. He was a white man from a small town in the South who loved my Spanish mother but could do without her half-black children. Racial slurs were a norm to him. This period strained my relationship with my

Take a pause to appreciate
how far you've come.

mother—a woman who loved her children dearly but had deep unprocessed pain of her own that was clouding her judgment. She would detest her husband's behavior one day, with great apologies to me, and then dismiss it on another day. I never knew which type of day it would be. My time with my mother back then was in sharp contrast to the safe, functional, and comforting home life my father was providing for me. This was the epitome of low vibrations versus high vibrations—in full effect.

These collective experiences created deep depression in me as a child, teen, and young adult. I experienced regular stomachaches, poor digestion, anxiety, shortness of breath, panic attacks, and fatigue, and I was underweight. I acquired what John Bradshaw calls in his book *Homecoming: Reclaiming and Healing Your Inner Child* a "spiritual-wound." I could never make sense of why I was so torn and at home in both worlds—one of the spiritual path of progress with my father and the other of pain and anxiety with my mother.

Later in life, the dots connected for me, and everything made sense. I came to see that my past had to be exactly what it was. The purpose and deep passion within me today that I use to advocate for higher potential living and healing for others are only possible because of the sum total of my combined past experiences—from trauma and pain to love, joy, and spirituality; from (family) financial struggle to affluence. I can relate to all of it.

But it would take years for me to realize this, as there would first be great mountains to survive and overcome.

Dark Night of the Soul

By the time I was in my early twenties the damage—although I was unaware of it at the time—began to reveal itself. It was showing up in my choices. For instance, it showed up in the relationship I was in, which turned into a domestic violence nightmare of two years until I escaped in the middle of the night. I had internalized the wrong messages—that pain and abuse were norms. I already had a low sense of self-worth, which led me to accept such an abusive relationship in the first place, but the effects of that abuse diminished whatever little amount of self-worth I had left. At the time, I was emptied out, or so I thought, and I couldn't untangle myself from the effects.

After escaping that abusive relationship, I found myself disoriented and hopeless, to the point of trying to end my life. I couldn't figure out how to make the pain and its negative patterns stop. But as fate would have it, my past, the pain, and the suicide attempt would not win, or have the final say. After I attempted suicide, I was unconscious for three days, and after regaining consciousness, my first reaction while in this dazed state was anger because I was still alive and, needless to say, unsuccessful in escaping the pain of my life. But then moments later, this other feeling and awareness rose within, and my focus shifted—into a comforting realization that my life had just been saved from ending in the tragic way it nearly did. The deep-rooted pain and duress that had been guiding and affecting my life for so long had not won.

13

The Divine does not
allow our pain or
dark nights to have
the final say.

Don't rush the
process. It takes time
returning to yourself.

Various spiritual teachings call this experience *the dark night of the soul*. It is a spiritual phenomenon originally coined by Spanish mystic-poet, priest, and saint Jose de le Cruz, widely known as John of the Cross, that happens to people to intentionally shake them awake, to activate their higher purpose, and to convert them and their lives into something new. As a spiritual practitioner and wellness educator, I've seen it many times. It's a temporary period of inner or spiritual crisis (although you don't realize it's temporary when you're in the midst of it) when the life you've come to know no longer makes sense, is no longer tolerable—often to the point of isolation and depression settling in.

My life had a divine appointment to not die physically, but spiritually and conceptually. My suicide attempt called for the death of the lifestyle, mindset, and cycle that were no longer serving me. For other people, the dark night of the soul may look different. It can be a more subtle and less intense experience that includes some pain and frustration, but no life trauma or spiritual crisis.

Both ways lead to awakening.

We see this in the case of Siddhartha Gautama, who—through his own dark night of the soul—later would become known to the world as the Buddha. Siddhartha was a beloved prince who lived a privileged and luxurious life. There was no initial life trauma or crisis in his case, but he became profoundly dissatisfied with his life and experienced an inner knowing and a tugging of his heart and soul toward a higher direction and purpose. For Siddhartha, this took the form of forsaking his royal life of privilege, giving it all up to reach enlightenment and higher purpose.

For me, this dark night reckoning was the beginning of something new. It led me to realizing that the slowly sprouting seeds planted deep within me all those years before—the ones that got me out of my unhealthy relationships and toxic life—were finally ready to break through and rise above the soil. Seeds germinate and grow only when the conditions are right, so having a new path that supported me in this way was essential.

Reconfiguration

We are all capable of starting over. Of vibrating higher daily. Of change. Of deciding what we give our energy and attention to, and what we don't. You may have journeyed into a traumatic dark night of the soul—lamented the death of a loved one, gone through heartbreak, experienced a loss of health or security; or you may have noticed a propelling higher call and force guiding you away from the life you've known. In all cases, you are always capable of the game-changing journey from death to rebirth into higher awakening.

Pain and suffering are most often the gateways and the initiation into our higher selves and higher purpose. These experiences usher the soul into transformation, into vibrating higher and experiencing empowerment. And then, into the unfolding of a new way of living, doing, and being in the world.

After my dark night of the soul, I started looking for solutions to overcome my circumstances instead of feeling defeated by them. The depression and shame that I quietly journeyed with throughout my childhood and teen years, and into adulthood, had consumed enough of my life. This dark night experience was a fork in the road, a turning point, an activation.

I was led and inspired to begin living more mindfully and intentionally through my everyday choices. And it started with what I ate. Food became the gateway. After some time and consistency, the vibrational awareness around how I had started eating soon grew and transferred to the types of energy I allowed into my environment, to how I managed my thoughts, to how I treated others and myself, to how I lived in general, and to the type of work I did in the world. One small decision and starting point led to a whole new way of being in the world—a better way for me. These various areas of my life had always been interconnected, but now I was living more and more aware of that interconnectedness, and I was more intentional in my day-to-day choices and decisions.

From mindful eating came awareness of bigger things. Thanks to a free Wednesday night support group for survivors of various forms of abuse, I learned to release my ego and my old way of thinking and surrender to necessary change—a wonderful thing for my soul. I continued deciding day after day and choice by choice to take my power and life back. Along the way, I had mentors, who each saw something more in me than what I—with my limited, yet changing, perspective at the time—saw in myself. I saw a victim and survivor; they saw someone overcoming adversity, a teacher and a hero.

My first full-on mentor was a calm, wise, older man called simply Dr. B. He entered my life by divine appointment, and my life has never been the same since. We met one warm summer afternoon in 2007 during what first appeared to be another random friendly meeting at a Whole Foods Market in Los Angeles. Our paths first crossed in the crowded store when we bumped into each other in passing. He was very courteous, we both laughed, and then we went our separate ways.

About ten minutes later I was standing perplexed in one of the supplement aisles—mind you, I was still new to healthy living at that time—struggling to choose a product. The struggle was real, and I hadn't the slightest clue what to choose. And then, as if divinely timed to precision, this gray-haired man who had bumped into me ten minutes earlier passed by, recognized the lostness in my posture, and intervened. This act of kindness turned into a twenty-minute conversation of great value. I was resonating deeply with the knowledge that this nice stranger was sharing with me. So much so that by the end of our exchange, he declared to me, "You're one of us. You're here on a mission and you're powerful. It's time to remember who you are."

For more than a decade, I've passionately and diligently worked with this mentor and others on my spiritual journey and path to vi-

It's time to rise into your empowerment and purpose. And though you may be scared and have repeatedly doubted yourself, surrender to the path. Realize that being trapped in fear is more exhausting and frustrating than moving forward into the unknown and your empowerment. Journey beyond those voices within that are discouraging you— the ones that may say you can't rise above wherever you are or have been. Open up to a new and better expression of your life.

brational awareness. These important and positively impactful connections would eventually guide my being toward teaching others
the path that has reconfigured me and my life, vibrationally.

Vibrate Higher Daily

Shaped throughout the reconfiguration process, I was able to
grow, learn, and unfold into my more authentic self—over time.
I leaned my whole life in a more healing, holistic direction. Like
sunflowers—which, no matter where they are planted, turn toward
the sun—I too began turning in the direction that nourished me.
This path has since become a way—no matter where I may find
myself planted—to turn toward the sun, the light.

Over the next decade, my journey to deeper healing, transformation, and discovery beyond the life and pain I'd known would be
through the path of what I call *vibrate higher daily*. Throughout this
book, I'll interchangeably refer to it as *the path*.

Things, people, and energies that were once painful memories
or blockages to my higher well-being and development were neutralized, including the limiting mindsets, tendencies, and habits that
I used to struggle with through my life. They no longer had power
or authority over my life. Living from this reality has been liberating
and life-changing.

My intention and prayer for you is to rise above and beyond
too—starting wherever you are. And also for you to step into your
empowerment and higher purpose. Whatever your story is, what-

Reflect on this for a moment:
some of the most beautiful,
empowering,
and fulfilling days of your life
are still out there—
all heading your way.
How divine!

ever your pain or disconnect from life may be, it's not allowed to have the final say in your life. Your story doesn't have to end where you feel it may be trying to end. Find your way through and beyond. Allow your pain and frustration to awaken and rebirth you into a new creation. From this inner space, you can create change within, reach your higher potential, and then help to shape a better society and world.

This is the life-shifting power of vibration, which is always within you. No matter where you are planted, may you always turn toward the sun.

WHAT IS VIBRATION?

So let's get into vibration! Besides being one of my favorite things to discuss, observe, and nurture, vibration is the constant bridge of communication between the mind, body, spirit, and outer world. This communication speaks through you and for you—and through and for all things surrounding you—at all times.

We mostly speak in
vibrations, not words.

How you communicate without saying a word, is through
vibration.

How you feel other people without them saying a word, is
through vibration.

How you discern whether a person, place, or thing is right for
you (or not right for you), is through vibration.

How you perceive the world around you, how you feel at any
given moment, and the state of your overall well-being—physical,
mental, spiritual, and emotional—is all vibration.

This is not just something you sense, feel, react to, and respond
to on a mind, body, spirit, emotional, or soul level; it is who and
what you are on a microscopic level. And it's also the state of your
overall well-being at any time. You are vibration expressing itself.
And human beings are not alone. Many beings throughout the ani-
mal, plant, and insect worlds base their communication and survival
on vibration. Three of my favorite beings, butterflies, elephants, and
whales, all use this force for communication. As do countless other
creatures. Vibration connects us all.

Even when it's not understood or recognized, vibration is there,
happening, and we're a part of it. For some people, like what I experienced, the awareness of this force could be buried under layers
of distraction, fear, pain, doubt, toxic cycles, shame, ego, religious
dogma—you name it. Yet we all have the potential to tap into the
vibrational field within us and around us. We can all live through
this vibrational awareness.

If you're new to it, like I was, it's about beginning wherever you are and however you can. Begin small if you have to, like I did. What started out as food awareness in my life, slowly grew and expanded into vibrational awareness.

The Whole Universe Operates Through Vibration

Everything in the universe is vibrating. Vibration is all around us, always within us, and always functioning. This can be seen on cellular, atomic, and microscopic levels: matter all around us may appear as one unified, individual thing, but under a microscope, it's all separate, and individual atoms, cells, and particles vibrate at certain frequencies. Even the cosmos. Our universe functions, communicates, and creates through this energy linking all things. Vibration is everything! For real!

When we become conscious of this life force within us and all things, we realize that we are not singular beings in silos alongside other singular beings and things: we are all connected. What happens outside of ourselves impacts us because vibration connects everything—like a superorganism. We live in a very symbiotic world and universe.

So not only are you a physical being; you are a vibrational being too. Your vibration changes based on the frequency—high or low—of your mindset, thoughts, actions, interactions, intentions, moods, and everything you come into contact with and consume.

As you become more
aware of and in tune
with your vibration,
your life begins to
harmonize.

("Good vibes" and "bad vibes"—yep, that same thing.) You know when you find yourself saying "I don't have a good feeling about this" or "I feel great about this"? Or when you say to someone "I feel low" or "I feel high"? That's vibration. Listen to it, feel it out. Pay attention to the vibes within you, around you, and in all things that influence you—spirit, mind, body, soul.

Another way we can look at vibes is in terms of harmony. Think of your favorite song. High vibes and positive energy are like hearing or feeling all the right notes. It's pleasing to the mind, body, and soul and can shift the atmosphere around you. Lower vibes and negative energy are like hearing the wrong notes played or sung out of tune. The right notes create harmony; the wrong notes cause disharmony and often become disturbing to the mind, body, soul, and atmosphere around you. Living out of harmony with our highest good creates stress, anxiety, compromised health, and unhealthy relationships in our personal lives, and war, fear, and hate in the larger world. Living in harmony with our highest good creates greater peace of mind, improved health, healthy relationships in our lives, and more peace, joy, and love in the world around us.

Whenever you find yourself feeling out of harmony and out of tune, find your note! Do more of what makes you vibrate higher and feel alive.

THE POWER
OF DAILY
AWARENESS

Vibrational-based living is the day-to-day lifestyle of intentionally moving through your life with awareness of forces operating from within you, through you, around you, and in all things. Vibrational-based living is transformative because it creates a shift in how you see, sense, connect with, and respond to everything within and around you. Living this way, though, takes living through daily vibrational awareness. And this starts the moment you awaken each day.

Everything around you is affecting your vibration. Even the subtle things. It could be clutter in a corner, in a sink, on a table or desk that you pass by which creates uneasy energy. Or perhaps the tone of news updates or social media claiming your early morning attention. It could be waking up with an "off" mood. Something as simple as setting up a morning routine that nourishes, fortifies, and positively aligns you—before the day carries you off in its various directions—makes a huge impact on the state of your energy and being for the rest of the day. Doing things early in the day that build up your high vibrational reserves is a great way to take charge and harmonize your day.

I emphasize the word *daily* in the term *vibrate higher daily* because this path is a process. The choices and the individual practices we adopt every day hold the power to shift us higher or lower. Through daily practices we are able to build a lifestyle that serves us and that supports our exodus from a life that doesn't serve us, personally and collectively. Just as running coaches will tell us that to become a runner we have to start slowly, with a mile a few times a week, so too we nurture vibrational-based living through small, incremental choices each day that build upon themselves. We are always creating our life through each moment and with each choice.

Create a Morning Routine

The potential for your life and future is shaped differently depending on whether you commit to unconscious habit and pattern or to vibrational awareness in your life. You always have the choice to exit autopilot mode, to clean out and update your mental programming; you have the freedom to create a new story.

Start your journey with a small step to that new story and daily awareness with a morning routine. Such routines are important because they lay the groundwork for your day, and ultimately your life—as days turn into weeks, weeks turn into months, and before you know it, months have become years. Setting a solid and supportive foundation for yourself through consistency, mindful behavior, persistence, and sustainable daily habits is key. And keep in mind that "consistency" here is not about perfection, but rather about progress, daily awareness, and noticeable results.

Take Inventory

What gives you good vibes? What gives you bad ones? You raise your vibration by implementing things in your life that are vibrationally therapeutic and fortifying and by omitting things that are not. You can do this through self-discipline, self-correcting, and guiding your mind and willpower. Think of professional athletes or martial arts masters. They operate with discipline through awareness of what will and will not fortify and sharpen their craft. That's vibrational awareness, and that's what can change your life. It's about knowing and honoring who and what supports you in being great. And knowing who and what does not. Only you can know and feel this.

Now that I realize my vibrations are speaking out through my thoughts, desires, and feelings, I poise myself differently than I used to. Living in awareness for me means embracing the opportunity for growth and self-mastery and persisting in a higher vibration when met with challenges and lower vibrational moments. Your vibration is like a muscle and a shield. The more you build it up, the stronger you are, and the stronger it is, as a result.

Guard Your Attention

With so many things competing for our attention in every waking hour, taking time for myself has become a nonnegotiable part of my spiritual practice. This keeps me more rooted and anchored throughout the various experiences of the day. And if I, for whatever reason, find myself feeling off balance or disconnected from myself, returning to the practice of slowing down and taking time out to vibrate higher puts me in tune and in balance again.

As you make your way through each day, keep in mind that it's not just food that is feeding you, but all energetic things around you. It's all affecting your state of being. Be aware of what you're vibrationally allergic or sensitive to. Just like with seasonal or food allergies, you'll know. Your body may respond—physically, with illness, a rash, a cold, a headache, a stomachache; or otherwise, with a blockage in some area of your life, an off mood, mental fog, or a sudden drop in energy levels or vibration. (More on this in the next chapter.) On the opposite end of the spectrum, stay aware and take note as to what is having a positive impact and effect on your spirit, mind, body, and soul. Pay attention to all of the signs coming from both ends of the spectrum. This is living and moving in vibrational awareness.

Self-Checks

Take time each day to check in with yourself to see how the at-mosphere, people, or things around you are affecting you. Also take time to become cognizant of how you're affecting everything around you, remembering that in certain cases, you could be the one out of harmony and throwing the vibes off. Staying aware in this way is key. When this has been the case in my own life, I've tried to snap out of it quickly, so as not to prolong the lower vibe and its effect on others and to get back in tune and harmony with my higher good. (I find the harmony. I find my note.) I try to stay mindful in the moment that I'd rather use positive reinforcement and energy over negative reinforcement and energy to bring about change or to manifest a better outcome. When things don't go my ideal way in the various aspects of my life, my awareness shifts to dealing with anything that may need to be dealt with, and then to keep moving forward—empowered, poised, and light—seeking to leave behind any lingering negative residue or vibes.

Know when to unplug from unproductive vibrations that show up in the various aspects of your life and cause disharmony or stagnation—in groups, in your home, in your relationships, during conversations, in public, or from within. You can always choose to conduct, reroute, or orchestrate your energy in a higher vibrational and more harmonious way. You hold this power within.

During my dark night of the soul, I went through the ultimate self-check. My life began breaking down and dismantling itself, which is one of the first stages in the spiritual process of awakening and transformation. My life had become too hard to live, but The Divine, still having purpose for this life of mine, intervened and rescued me. I decided that from then on, I would no longer go on living the way I had been living and that I definitely wasn't going to die that way either. This is when the pain that I journeyed with began to be converted into awakening, healing, and purpose.

The same potential is available and present in you, in both the large-scale moments and the more routine and mundane ones.

Certain things, implemented both in your daily life and beyond it, support you, heal you, and allow you to become more whole within. Becoming aware of the difference between low vibration and high vibration can mean the difference between moving toward or away from progress and wholeness.

As I've navigated life, this path cleansed and nurtured my heart, mind, body, and soul. It has allowed me to shift in ways I once never thought possible. It's been healing. It's been redeeming. It's helped me live with purpose and in a better direction. A whole new life became available to me. It's been the definition of daily grace.

And may it be so for you too, friend. Welcome to the journey, and the path, of vibrate higher daily!

SELF-ASSESSMENT

Let's Identify the Vibes

1. What's contributing to your current mood and vibration, and how?

2. Do you feel a sense of disorientation after eating a particular food or having contact with a particular person, place, or thing?

3. What choices and behaviors served you well or did not serve you well today or this week?

4. For what didn't serve you well, what corrective measures can you take?

5. Are there peak times of the day when you notice a shift in your vibration, both positive and not so positive? If so, when?

6. What can you begin doing to optimize your high vibrational peak times and nurture the not-so-high peak times?

Reflection Time

1. What is the vibrational quality of your overall well-being and life?

2. What raises your vibration and what lowers it?

3. Do a quick introspective scan of your habitual mindset, behaviors, character, habits, and lifestyle choices. Are they working for you, or against you?

4. Are you living toward your higher good, higher development, and healing, or away from them?

5. In what areas of your life do you feel a calling to transform and live in a higher way?

6. How have you, or how will you, honor the daily process of vibrating higher daily and vibrational-based living?

7. Is there anything holding you back from feeling free to vibrate higher daily?

8. What steps can you take to liberate yourself in order to move forward and thrive?

Vibrational Inventory

What kind of vibration are you reinforcing through your habits?

What kind of vibration are you reinforcing through the foods you eat?

What kind of vibration are you reinforcing through your daily lifestyle choices?

What kind of vibration is feeding and influencing you through the things you listen to, watch, read and consume mentally?

What kind of vibration is emanating from the relationships in your life?

What kind of vibration is emanating from the work you put out into the world?

What kind of vibration are you creating with the words you use about your life and yourself?

What kind of vibrations are you exposing yourself to?

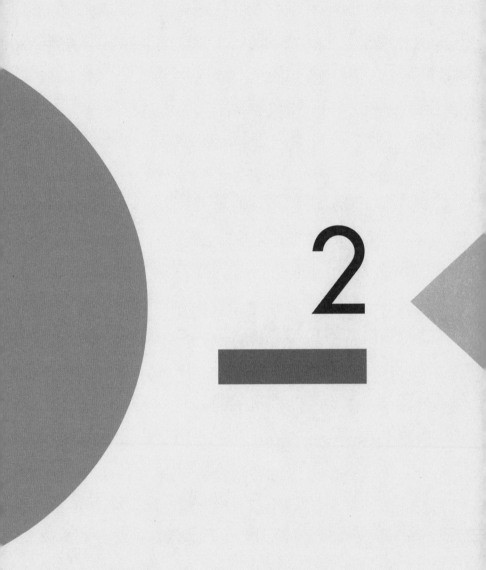

2

You're being guided.
Don't move forward with
people, plans, or opportunities
if the vibes aren't right.

Vibration matters because it's the root of ourselves. It's how we communicate internally and with the wider world around us, and it's how we sense and feel our way through wherever we find ourselves. It's the spiritual force always radiating through all created things. When you use this force for your higher good, you are able to more consciously and intentionally function and thrive in the world. Vibrations guide you when you're on a spiritual path. They guide you toward what's best for you and away from what isn't. They give direction for tuning out of a life that isn't serving you and tuning in to a life that will. Are you tuned in?

For a radio station to be heard clearly (and enjoyed

fully), the radio must be tuned to the correct frequency. This is the same for us. We are like human radios, and our bodies work like antennas that tune in to frequencies, pick up signals, and sense and communicate through vibration.

We are electrical beings. And even when we don't realize it, we are broadcasting and picking up signals continuously. Our vibration is always on, and we have to be tuned in to the correct frequency in order to function optimally; think clearly; heal properly; and offer, serve, and show up at our best.

Being aware of your personal vibration and how it contributes to your well-being and your energy toward others empowers you. Yes, it does! You see, when you find yourself out of tune, or off balance, you can *choose* not to remain trapped there, not to keep going along with whatever it may be and instead to counteract in order to neutralize the unharmonious forces influencing you.

This is what makes living with vibrational awareness so powerful: you're in control. You can change the dial and make any necessary adjustments. You can take your power back, clear away any static, and return to a state of equilibrium and harmony. Vibrational awareness is power!

- Are you thinking, living, and acting from a clear channel or from one that is out of tune and full of static?
- Are you in a harmonious state and environment? Or are you in one of disharmony and static?

THE
POWER
WITHIN

The power within you is divine. Yes, it's already there! You've got the indwelling power! You're prewired with the capability to decide in which direction you shift your energy and attention toward. The key is that you have to connect to this force within you. Vibrational awareness practices, such as harmonizing yourself with what serves you and disconnecting from what doesn't, change the trajectory of your life. Allow vibrational awareness to be the operating system of your life. Embrace it so you can overcome whatever it is that burdens your heart, stresses your mind, challenges your strength, weighs your spirit down, or hinders your way forward.

Most of us have some *it* or *them* that causes us imbalance or pain: negative self-talk, the unharmonious actions of a loved one, a toxic association or interaction that triggers us, or a destructive cycle or habit we're quietly (or not so quietly) trying to shake for the umpteenth time. Nevertheless, we can choose to no longer live on the terms set by *it* or *them*.

Let's look at how. First, you stop living on autopilot. You stop vibrating at the same frequency of *it* or *them*. You stop resonating with *it* or *them*. You stop reinforcing *it* or *them* through your choices and actions. You stop identifying yourself with *it* or *them*, and instead you begin to vibrate into a new awareness, perspective, consciousness, intention, and personal power. You tune out *it* or *them* in order to tune in to what better serves you and resonates with you. Basically, you stop harmonizing with *it* or *them*.

Think of times when you no longer felt compelled to pursue certain friendships, social circles, or relationships—the ones that were growing more and more unharmonious to you. Or the times when you experienced yourself outgrowing an environment—your atmosphere at work or a particular line of work, a location, your personal space, a belief system, a group mentality, or a habit. Think, too, of a time when you decided to take your power back from a breakup that caused, or nearly caused, an emotional meltdown. These are all times when—no matter how easier-said-than-done it was—*you did it*. You vibrated out of what was no longer serving you and no longer vibrationally good for you in terms of energy and environment. You were connected to your indwelling power. Yes! That's it! You were *living your power*! You've got to acknowledge and celebrate that! More of this in your life, when and where necessary!

Mindset is how

vibration speaks.

THE
JOURNEY

You are the hero of your life. And along the way, you're going to experience your own hero's journey of unfolding into a vibrationally aware and higher potential being in the world. On the path, there comes a time when a higher voice steps in to lead the way—teaching you how to be whole again, and maybe for what feels like the first time, how to live out your higher potential and purpose in the world. Farther and farther you'll move away from what you've known, and out into the great unknown.

You Are a Vibrational Being

Staying aware of the vibrations within you and within all the things you come into contact with is essential to honoring yourself as a vibrational being because these are the things that either feed you or deplete you *every day*. This is the undercurrent of life, health, progress, and transformation. A great indication of where you are vibration-wise is to become aware of your mental and emotional states at any given time. The more in charge you are of your life vibrationally, the less the world around you is able to take charge and control of you.

Don't ever stop believing
in your personal
transformation.
It is happening even on the
days you may not realize it
or feel like it.

Vibrating higher daily is how you take your power back— on all levels.

The beginning of this journey is about implementing higher vibrational routines, habits, and practices into your everyday life. Embracing such daily rituals could include and mean that you now:

- Take time to nurture and recenter yourself.
- Slow down and relax into your life more.
- Go within yourself and emit more grace and love.
- Have a very necessary cup of tea, massage, hug, herbal tonic, or laugh.
- Prepare and have a nourishing meal (in peace and joy, and undistracted).
- Take time to recuperate to clear away any vibrational buildup you've accumulated and absorbed during the day.
- Allow all stress or worries to wither away through vibrational work, such as spirit-care and self-care.
- Devote yourself to Do Not Disturb time and proper rest.
- Connect to the positive things and people that harmonize and balance you and renew your strength.

Remember Who You Are: The Hero

Live in the awareness of who you are and where you're headed on your journey. During the complexities of life, heroes rise to meet the challenges. Heroes often tap into a higher power and ability within themselves to fulfill their journey. And although this power and ability at times are tested, a higher guiding force is at work, which means any defeat is temporary. This guiding force allows heroes to pass through all types of terrain and weather in an otherworldly way. Staying aligned and connected to this higher source of power, come what may, is the way of the hero. Alignment and connection happen through fortification, including taking care of spirit, body, and mind, as well as nutrition and environment.

The first step to victory begins with remembering that you are the hero of your life each day.

Joseph Campbell's famous 1949 book, *The Hero with a Thousand Faces*, illuminates the rites of passage that we all go through to become the hero of our own lives on the spiritual, psychological, and personal levels. In the 1988 PBS special titled *The Power of Myth*, Campbell shared with host Bill Moyers the basic motif of the hero's journey—leaving a state of psychological dependence and entering into psychological self-responsibility. This, Campbell says, requires a death and resurrection, in which the hero leaves one condition and sets off to find the "source of life" in order to bring herself or himself forth in a richer and more mature condition in the world. Hero myths, according to Campbell, are about the transformation of consciousness.

This is what the journey of transformation, reconfiguration, and vibrating higher daily is all about. It's doing the work of transforming into the hero of your life, becoming empowered, and becoming a higher vibrational being within yourself and out in the world.

Environment

The journey starts with leaving your current physical and emotional state—either willingly or unwillingly. This looks different for everyone: sometimes it's up and leaving a physical place or situation of comfort; sometimes it's outgrowing a relationship; sometimes it's altering your current surroundings or mindset to better serve you—but always it's about exploring and answering the call that's summoning you forward, higher, and beyond the places you've been.

Like all living organisms, we thrive best in the right environment. Plants need sunlight and water for photosynthesis. Babies and children need nurturing, nourishment, and shelter. A person who is ill or in recovery needs rest, healing foods, and peace and quiet, known in the medical and wellness field as a healing environment. The right atmosphere and conditions matter to all things. Do you know what the proper environment is for you? The right space will nourish you, help you grow, and support your process—that's how you'll know and recognize it. The right environment is a safe space to pull your life together, restore, and move forward.

If you notice that the "seed" within you isn't growing where you're planted, it's time to move to more fertile ground.

Reflect on your environment. Is it a place of stability in your life? Is it enriching? This goes for thoughts, people, and spaces—they're all environments.

You deserve a place that nourishes you and where you're able to anchor yourself for a while and get what you need. This stability

Evaluating where
you are is always a
necessary part of the
process.

helps to sustain you, on a soul level, in living a transformative life, a higher vibrational life.

Sometimes you'll have to be gentle with yourself and realize that it's not you or anything you're doing wrong—it's the environment you're in. It's not allowing you to thrive. It's not what makes you grow, heal, flourish, thrive, and expand. It's not fertile ground for the seed within you.

Switching environments is key when your inner environment is right but your outer environment is all wrong. This can look like switching environments altogether, or re-creating a better one where you are. This re-creating is done by shifting the atmosphere and harmonizing your space (in order to raise its vibration). Shifting your atmosphere is about filling the air around you with a better force, vibration, and power. This takes dedication and consistency because, you know, old habits stick. Breaking habits deserves its own Broadway show—it can be emotional, comical, adventurous, and ultimately applaudable. So even when you're the only person both onstage and in the audience, do the work, and cheer for yourself all along the way.

Here are some of the many ways to shift and harmonize your atmosphere:

- Pay attention to your home and space, because whatever is in your everyday view matters.

- Make sure everything in your space nourishes, serves, and supports you, from the placement of furniture to the pictures on your walls to the food in your pantry and fridge to the items on your nightstand.

- Since all things and objects carry a vibration, let go of what is creating disharmony. Decluttering and cleansing your space are purifying spiritual practices.

- Changing your space doesn't always have to be big. You can start small, making incremental, yet noticeable, shifts where and how you can.

- Saturate the atmosphere with relaxing music and the aroma of your favorite balancing essential oils, incense, candles, and burning woods.

- Place inspiring, beloved things where you can easily see them.

- Take five minutes each morning to set the intention for your interaction that day with life, your environment, and your goals.

- Realize when a space has become toxic and take the necessary steps to correct it, or to remove yourself and cleanse from it.

- Stay open to positive and necessary solutions and change.

- Be kind and gentle with yourself in the process.

The Building Blocks of Transformation + Transmutation

Initiation

Like in a cocoon, the sacred space where a caterpillar becomes a butterfly, being in the right environment during metamorphosis and rebirth is essential. During the transformation process, in the most divinely organized and necessary ways, your life—much like the caterpillar's—will begin to self-destruct. This dismantling initiates the transformation process, offering you access into a new way of being in the world. A new life. Your small daily decisions about what you give your attention and energy to start to add up: maybe you replace the phone or laptop on your nightstand with a book of daily devotions so you start your mornings by reading affirmations instead of looking at a screen. Maybe you start a regular practice of calling a relative or close friend once a week instead of giving your time and energy to people who continually drain you. Or maybe you decide to no longer fear the transformation process, but instead to surrender, to trust, and to open your whole self up to it.

After a while, your life will begin to mirror your higher vibration. Your new state of being will become more visible, and stable, to yourself and to others around you, and you'll find yourself being more poised and empowered during life moments that used to intimidate you (or trigger you). Your transformation will begin to be reflected in your communication, your character, your posture, your choices, your works and creativity, and in how you perceive and interact with your inner and outer worlds. On your transformation journey, no matter where you find yourself, and no matter what amount of strength you have within you, always shift the focus to vibrating higher. Think of it as your control or command center, a place you draw higher support, empowerment, and awareness from to help you manage your life.

By living in this heightened state of awareness, you move away from an ordinary life that is not interested in your higher good. And slowly but surely, the unhelpful toughest parts within you divinely begin to weaken, to break up, and then to dissolve over time. The visible and invisible barriers you've experienced, and may experience, along your journey will have less of a lasting effect on you. You will break free of it all by living from a higher and more harmonious energy and empowered state of mind.

The transformation and transmutation process is one of the most powerful stages of the journey. During the period of my early life when I was on the wrong vibrational path, my younger self had no idea of the healing and higher potential that was possible for me. Because of that, my twenties were an all-out mess: I was mixed up with the wrong people, I was violated and abused, and, as I've shared, I felt stuck to the point of thinking suicide was the best option out. My life on many days was a full-out war, and I suffered from post-traumatic stress syndrome because of it. My self-worth was depleted. I had no clue that the new woman I am today, and

Vibrating higher during transformation brings you back home to yourself, over and over again.

Grapes must be
crushed to make wine.

Diamonds form
under pressure.

Olives are pressed
to release oil.

Seeds grow
in darkness.

Whenever you feel crushed, under
pressure, or in darkness,
you're in a powerful place for
transformation and transmutation.

the strength that I have and the work that I now do, was inside of me. It was completely beyond my vision. And I had no clue then that no matter what was going on, seeds of change were within me—and they had been there all along. The soil was so thick that I couldn't see them. It wasn't until I began to wander away to seek a different path for myself, and to begin working on moving in a healing and whole direction, that my life met with a new reflection and potential. It was an uphill battle on some days, a calm walk on others, but most of all it was about journeying through the various terrains of life to experience glorious transformation.

Doing the Work with Consistency

First things first: reaching higher levels of self-development takes doing the work with consistency. Doing the work is not always easy, but it's how you get to where you're going. Transformation occurs because of daily choices and actions over a steady amount of time in a consistent direction.

As you take on the mission and call of transforming your life, remember to be patient while honoring the process. Stay committed to your development when the process gets complex and difficult. During various seasons and terrains of life, times may come when it will appear easier to quit or settle for good enough. But through perseverance, you will allow the process of transformation to complete its necessary cycle and purpose within you and your life.

Transformation also
looks like this: examining
ourselves for growth and
leaving nothing out of
our examination.
Let's look at it all.

Getting Unstuck + Moving in the Right Direction

At various points in our journey toward attaining vibrational awareness, we can find ourselves stuck, unable to move forward, unable to get beyond. Transforming our life and getting it to progress in a better direction takes new and intentional moves. In order to move in any direction from where we've been, a dominant guiding vibration has to be present, and chosen.

This is like Newton's first law of motion, or the law of inertia: the only way to change an object that's stuck in place or stuck in the same continuous motion is to introduce a more powerful force.

Early in my journey, my strategy for getting unstuck was releasing people from my life who didn't serve my higher good. And I would instead spend more and more time around mentors and like-minded people who nurtured me and inspired me to grow, heal, and live in my power. This was the more powerful force—the guiding vibration—that confronted my inertia and helped me get unstuck. I've carried that through all of my life to this day: I know what makes me feel like my harmonious self, and I turn to those people and things when I notice a lower vibrational state, pattern, or loop sprouting up. I let go of what doesn't serve me and make space for what does through taking deliberate, intentional, and necessary action.

Life and its journey will take us in the direction of our dominant thoughts, actions, and vibration, so choose wisely and with awareness. When we do this, we take our power back. This is when we begin to sense and realize whether our current environment (direction, place, relationships, and mindset) is serving us. This is how and where our vibration becomes a tool and a vehicle to shift us from one path and move us onto a new (and better) one.

Lock In

Find what works! Explore, discover, and witness what is effective in your environment and zero in on that dominant vibration. Being energetically locked in requires what's known as *holding your vibration*, which brings us back to being consistent. Locking in to vibrations that serve you—from time spent with supportive friends to a morning walk to nourishing foods to a spiritual practice—is a key part of transitioning and transforming because without holding your vibration, you'll experience a yo-yo effect; that is, the winds of life can blow you in random directions with no real or lasting stability or destination in sight. Holding a positive, agreeable, and focused vibration is essential to transformation and vibrating higher daily. Holding a negative, disagreeable, unfocused, or ego-dominant vibration is counterproductive to transformation and going higher.

Following my mother's return to the spirit world in 2018, grief was a sticky terrain for me to journey through. After some time had passed, I recognized that I needed a steady energy to lock in to. My soul's medicine came through various yet interconnected channels of heart, body, mind, and spirit. The parents of my best friend,

Asiya, offered me their dreamy home in the beautiful Southern California hills as a place of refuge. They invited me to stay there, offering to cook and care for me while I wrote this book. "Come and write here," they said. "You can sit among the trees, flowers, canyons—stay as long as you need to."

The vibration of this offering touched me deeply. It was the force of kindness in action. Locking in to the mere thought of it helped me to get through one of the most tender and heart-wrenching seasons and terrains of my life.

Self-balancing and self-correcting are core principles of vibrational-based living. Every system and organ in your body does this to maintain equilibrium and alignment. May you do it also on conscious, emotional, and vibrational levels. Persistently holding your vibration keeps your heart, mind, and life in balance and returns them to a state of equilibrium when they are caught off guard, blindsided by life, or stray from balance. Read the signs so that you don't continue in the wrong direction or end up stuck on the side of your journey's road. Recognize when to move and exit the route—and then move and exit the route.

Introspection

Introspection is about getting to the core of your being and understanding yourself in a nonjudgmental way. Stop to reflect and look within. Take a genuine look at what's inside, while loving yourself through whatever you find there, the good and the not so good; this is the higher vibrational way. Self-love is a powerful force to implement in the process of growing, transforming, and vibrating higher daily.

In the wake of my mother's transition, I was in need of introspection. I spent a lot of quality time with my sweet sister, Aisha, who also follows the path of vibrational-based living. She and I talked, cried, laughed, grieved, and healed together. We nurtured each other, and together we found our way through. Thanks to Aisha's recommendation, I also took time to look within my body to recognize and release all of the stagnated tension and grief that I had accumulated within. I turned to what nourishes me. I took nourishing baths in Epsom salts, herbs, and essential oils; I got massages; and I also did a new thing: I introduced my body to reflexology, a practice that has since stuck and become highly essential. Staying open to what the many aspects of your being may need—your heart, mind, body, spirit, and soul—is a powerfully integrative way to practice introspection and take real good care of yourself.

Introspection helps you not only to heal, but also to become more self-aware. There was a point on my journey where I realized through introspection that in times of stress, a "fix me" mentality would often arise. I'd look to others to fix me, to make me feel whole, yet I realized it never worked or lasted for long. I had to rise in this area. I had to embrace my power and fix myself. I had to become who I was waiting for. While other people can be a valuable support system and cheer us on, it's ultimately up to us to do the necessary work, to do our part.

Whatever requires developing, transcending, releasing, maturing; whatever needs more grace, love, forgiveness, work, and more time to process and heal—introspection through self-love is the way.

Empowerment

Empowerment is a vital part of the process to not shy away from or bypass, but arrive at, vibrate into, and live from. As we do the work to let go, heal, recover, vibrate higher, and transform, that's not the end of the process. It's vital to not stop or remain stuck and stagnant in the process or somewhere on the journey due to not reaching empowerment. Living life from a place of power is what vibrating higher daily is all about. Empowerment allows us to live from a more whole, connected, and authentic place.

For me, empowerment meant taking authority over my life, taking my power back, and recognizing and trusting that my gifts were connected to my healing and life's work in the world. Empowerment meant choosing to vibrate higher daily—through whatever came my way. By letting go of what didn't serve me, stepping forward to do my work in the world, and sharing my gifts, I stopped allowing fear to be a comfort zone and a place where I remained stuck and unempowered.

Let's empower ourselves—mind, body, heart, and soul—and rise higher—emotionally, vibrationally, spiritually, culturally, and socially!

Lurking Within | Residue

Transformation comes by not expecting yourself to be perfect during the process, or "complete" before due time, but rather by rising above, getting better, gaining ground, and vibrating higher—daily, wherever and whenever necessary.

That being expressed, sometimes no matter how much work you have done, or healing you have sought, the old self is still lurking within and may at times be triggered to rise up within you and show itself. This is the residue of your past, not the new you. It may try to rise again from within and gain control over your mind, body, and experiences—and whatever else it can. Keep clearing away the residue by staying on the path. Staying consistent and persistent is what renews you and finally dissolves the former self. The former self you've outgrown, or are in the process of outgrowing, can no longer be in control or thrive and survive on your new progressive energy and vibration. At last! So keep clearing your way.

Be aware that things can get messy when you start to clean up and transform your life. But life has a sense of humor, and after you've been through this process a number of times, the messy parts can start to seem comical to you and feel less disastrous. Thank goodness! This helps you stay light within and journey in balance—because the highs and the lows are real. The journey, life, and the whole world are an orchestra of high and low notes. Knowing how to harmonize and conduct your life well is essential.

TERRAINS WE JOURNEY THROUGH

The journey itself is a sacred and necessary part of the process, not to skip. And yet it can be difficult to surrender to and begin. This section is to mentally prepare you for the journey ahead, where eventually you may find yourself immersed in one of the many terrains of life and journeying. Preparation allows you to more readily accept the mission and proceed with skill and higher awareness. And after a while, you don't just "try" living from a new vibration, you begin to *own it,* and the path becomes doable, effective, and rewarding. A new you comes into being. Praise be!

The not-so-easy parts of life are part of the journey too, and this is where a lot of people come to a halt and are tempted to quit. Sometimes they do quit, or resist, tune out, or lose hope. But in order to arrive where you're going, you have to keep going—through the different terrains—to the other side. Our ability to accept the mission and do the necessary work to get through is life-altering.

The daily process is not about chasing perfection; it's about ris-

Love yourself through it.

You deserve to pour your
whole self into the process.

ing every day from wherever you find yourself and becoming better, doing better, from that place.

When the journey is long, journey fatigue, burnout, mental exhaustion, and a need for recovery may arise. And through and through, I've found that it's higher purpose, my spirituality, and honoring my self-care routine that empower me to overcome those things. I can continue to move through, while no longer being overcome or hindered by the process.

Think of a long road trip. You leave a familiar place behind, often traveling through unfamiliar wilderness to get to where you're going. You're patient through the middle journey, knowing that you'll arrive in due time. This allows you to relax and flow into the process. Life, spirituality, and your journey all operate in this same way. And although at times you may feel that you have no road map, the way becomes visible as you begin journeying.

The Metaphorical Terrains

The Mountain

The mountain is your obstacle. It's the thing that feels overwhelming to get around or over. It often causes stress and lower vibrations. The mountain is the emotional heaviness: the burdens, pain, stressors, triggers, obstacles, workload, lifestyle, habits, and people that don't serve your higher good. It's your not-so-positive habits and cycles that are stuck on repeat. It's whatever you're currently stressing about or losing sleep over. It's the thing you feel like you might have a nervous breakdown over. That's your mountain.

Vibrating higher is climbing the mountain. As you start moving up, you're able to see life from higher vantage points. With the advantage of higher perspective, you're more aware of your surroundings; your insight is expanded; and the things you once thought were large become smaller, more viable, surmountable, or at times insignificant to you.

On the journey, everyone has to climb and overcome their mountains.

Purpose of the mountain: The journey brings you to the mountain to strengthen and fortify you, to raise your awareness, to expand your vision, and to build vibrational and spiritual muscle, endurance, and resilience. The mountain is the entry point to self-discipline, renewed strength, and higher awareness, insight, and perspective.

The Desert

The desert is the place on your journey where it appears you're alone (although technically and spiritually, you're not). When you're in the desert, nothing seems to be growing or moving toward you. Nothing appears nourishing. The desert is the period when you're forced to be away from the norm. It's a wilderness experience when you don't see *it* manifesting or getting nearer. Boredom, loneliness, and even hopelessness can set in if you're not watchful.

The desert is also a place where things and people are divinely stripped away. It's a space of solitude, release, and reflection that can—if you vibrate higher through it—become a paradise and oasis. This powerful place of deep refuge is a resting place where you can experience transformation, awakening, and rebirth. The desert is a space of purging and allows for higher connection and alignment with The Divine: it's oftentimes a place of lasting spiritual significance.

Everyone has to journey through their own desert experience.

Purpose of the desert: The desert is the transitional place in the journey where you purge all that you are not and dissolve all that's no longer useful. It is the initiation and entry point into a new vibration of you and your life's purpose, power, and work—the place through which you become your truer and higher self.

The Storm

A spiritual storm is a divinely controlled experience, event, or condition in your life that can cause loss, confusion, and pain. Yet this chaos is for your higher good and progress. The storm is where and when some level of your life is suddenly disrupted by the winds of change. As a result, you can feel hopeless and left with no sense of direction or escape. Further disorientation and losing of the way can set in if you're not careful and aware of the powerful purpose of this metaphorical weather.

Vibrating higher is how you can outlast the storm. While in its midst, you vibrate higher by seeking shelter in, aligning with, and anchoring yourself in The Divine. Drawing nearer to The Divine, a greater force, gives you spiritual covering and leads to insight, strength, direction, and the perfect peace that holy scriptures speak of. Through the storm, and afterward, as you move onward, you gain greater resilience and power.

Remember that you're never alone in the storm and that it has a greater working purpose in your life. This perspective allows you to endure and outlast the storm in a more empowered way. As a result, the storm elevates you to higher levels within, opening the way for a new direction and higher stability in your life.

Storms have three stages: the developing storm, the mature storm, and the dissipating storm. Knowing this and recognizing when you're entering or leaving each stage helps you to remain prepared. Keep in mind that all storms pass, the skies clear, and the sun comes out again.

Calming and stilling your mind is a spiritual tool that plays a huge part in calming and stilling the storm.

Since the storm is not a physical terrain like the mountain and the desert, it can happen at any time during the journey. This is a trademark of its unstable nature. It can happen in any terrain. When this happens, you may find yourself feeling not only alone, but also temporarily overwhelmed.

Physical storms and spiritual storms are both created by unstable atmospheres, but they also help stabilize the atmosphere. Whatever is hindering you from moving forward, the storm comes to clear the way through necessary cleansing and purification. Remember during the storm that this too shall pass.

Everyone has to journey through and outlast their own storms.

Purpose of the storm: The journey brings you to the storm to strengthen you, to clear your path, and to reroute your life. The storm purifies you and helps you develop a higher level of spiritual, mental, and emotional stability and power.

The Ocean

Life happens in tides and waves. The ocean is a spiritual metaphor for the state and vastness of your emotions and energy. It's the unexplored depths of your subconscious mind, your potential, and the current vibration of your life.

Waves represent your inner life—your emotions, vibrations, energy, and moods. Your waves are what you, at any given moment, vibrationally feel and express. Your ocean speaks through your reactions, behaviors, choices, moods, and words.

In the course of each day, the waves come and go to the shores of your life moment by moment, experience by experience, and tide by tide.

Tides represent your outer life, the surrounding stimuli that affect your inner waves, such as the people, foods, and energies you come into contact with. Tides show up as either high vibrations or low vibrations and vary in intensity (like high tide and low tide). Tides are the experiences and circumstances that, with skill, you navigate into, through, and then out of.

The various ocean states represent the sliding scale of joy and turbulence in your life. Like the ocean, you are capable of being peaceful, calm, soothing, stable, focused, and balanced as well as stormy, overpowering, unstable, unpredictable, unfocused, and imbalanced.

The ocean is about maintaining higher awareness and balance within and without so that you don't feel unbalanced or disoriented to the point of sinking too deep. When the mind is at a higher vibration, the ocean within is a place of empowerment, refuge, and relaxation. When the mind is vibrating lower, it's a place of disempowerment, turbulence, and vibrational imbalance. Emotional waves can obstruct your vision and hinder your ability to navigate forward successfully and clearly in life. When in balance, your emotions support your vision, progress, and movement forward, birthing greater strength, courage, and faith along the way.

Everyone has to journey through and cross their own ocean.

Purpose of the ocean: The journey brings you to the ocean to gain inner balance and peace. The ocean moves you into higher levels of balance and self-control. This terrain also relaxes, restores, and purifies you during the process. The ocean washes to shore what no longer serves you. It's up to you to release what goes to shore. Instead of holding on to what comes up, detach and allow the ocean to wash "it" away. This is how the ocean seeks to initiate you into strength and higher vibrations.

The Fog

In the fog, you can't see your way clearly, you feel stuck, and you may have to slow down or stop to regain clarity and greater insight. When you're in fog, your path can be clouded by fear, distraction, stress, and exhaustion. Other people and doubt may distract you, and you may find yourself experiencing spiritual heaviness and low vibrations.

As you vibrate higher, the fog eventually clears and you break out of any stagnation and blockage in your life. You're able to move forward. Sometimes you have to break from the norm, try something new, and practice lots of self-care to defog your mind and life. But like a lighthouse, you can shine through the fog by seeking the light of The Divine and the light within.

If you're not aware of and in tune with the purpose of this metaphorical weather, you may find yourself making impulsive and reactionary conscious or unconscious decisions.

Like the storm, the fog is not a terrain but rather a state that can happen at any place along the journey. For example, you might discover a period of feeling immersed in fog when you approach your mountain, and when this happens you are left feeling both perplexed and overwhelmed by the obstacle in front of you.

Everyone has to clear away and overcome their own fog.

She emerged

through it all

transformed.

Purpose of the fog: The journey brings you to the fog to gain greater clarity, to purify your mind, to release what isn't serving you, and to offer better focus and direction. It's about finding your higher way—through.

Overcoming the Terrains

When you're growing into higher vibrations, your ability to overcome metaphorical terrains and weather becomes a spiritual art. You'll become more and more skilled and masterful. No longer will you be defeated by what comes; you'll know it's a sacred and positive process that you're called to journey through. This is essential on the journey, and it makes all the difference between feeling overwhelmed versus feeling like all is in divine order and you're more than capable. You'll remember you're the hero. You'll be more and more poised and in your power.

We're each here to prevail over the terrains of our lives, in spite of it all, and to accomplish what we're sent to do. Vibrating higher is how we do it. Apply and integrate all the necessary tools that you learn along the way. When you find yourself journeying through a metaphorical terrain or weather, know that it's only temporary. It's an invitation to vibrating higher daily. And each is a gateway, an initiation process for transformation, elevation, fortification, and higher purpose.

Whatever terrain you're currently in, see it as a sacred place, a strengthening place, and a resting place. Rest into the process and honor what it has come to do for you.

THE WISDOM AND REWARDS WE GAIN ALONG THE WAY

Vibration Instead of Gratification

We cross emotional mountains, oceans, and deserts to come back to ourselves. Back to a place to recognize what matters to us. In the end, we let go of the need for instant gratification and embrace something deeper and more lasting.

For much of my life, I chose food, entertainment, relationships, and experiences that gratified me on one level but ultimately lowered my vibration on another. My kitchen was Junk Food Central, I loved a good toxic television show or movie, I could repeat every last lyric of my once favorite (but now too offensive) rap songs, and unfulfilling friendships and toxic relationships were my daily reality (extra thanks to The Divine for this transformation). I was going along with what I figured was right for me at the time, while also knowing it wasn't right for me in the long run. This is how most of the modern world around us is set up: gratification instead of vibration. What would the world look like if we lived the reverse?—vibration instead of gratification.

If we aren't careful, gratification can give us a false sense of something being right for us. Or it can make us feel fulfilled, but only on a surface level, leaving the deeper parts of us malnourished. The allure of gratification often leads us to living an impulsive life, not an intentional one. And if we are not living an intentional life, we aren't living toward our higher potential. Higher potential is real and lasting gratification. Not living in the direction of our higher potential causes the opposite of gratification: disappointment. This is how things can appear right for us and then leave us feeling unfulfilled once the confetti settles.

A point came in my journey where this stopped being okay with my spirit. I was over and done with living a life distracted by confetti. And if there was going to be confetti, I wanted to feel just as fulfilled after it settled and was swept away.

There was a time during my twenties when I would play small and dim my light. I'd do this so the people around me would feel comfortable in some way or another. And for a time I'd feel a (false) sense of belonging and acceptance (the gratification thing). But living from this vibration, although it gratified me, was doing the opposite in my soul—it was lowering my vibration. As I continued giving my power away, I was attracting more low vibrational experiences, people, and relationships. And that's the unharmonious and problematic thing about false or instant gratification.

How can something be
pleasurable and yet no good
for us at times, leaving us
worse off and empty?

Our vibration dictates daily
what side of life we are on.

During that time I was living life at a low altitude and experienced much turbulence as a result. Think about air travel. Planes that travel a short distance fly low, and as a result they experience more turbulence. Making the journey is unpleasant and even distressing. On the other hand, planes that fly a longer distance fly high, above the turbulence, resulting in a smoother ride, a better experience, and a more pleasant journey.

This is also how vibration works and why it matters. The lower you vibrate, the more turbulence and chaos you experience on your journey, and the progress and change you experience are also shorter lived. The higher you vibrate, the more pleasant your journey, and the route leads to long-term and lasting progress and change. Vibrating higher alters the trajectory of your life and its experiences.

Now that I know better, I do better. These days, I go straight for vibration and navigate and aim higher.

Mind, Body, Vibration Connection

When you're living in a way that's more in tune with your personal vibration and what affects it and how so, your whole self experiences greater healing, peace, relaxation, creativity, and clarity. Through vibrating higher daily you gain more control of your mind and are able to overcome moments that would usually deplete you spiritually, emotionally, and energetically. Through reaching higher vibrations within, you rebound and find your center and your balance much more quickly, and you function in your power and higher potential more consistently.

Often in my past, a huge sticky place for me was taking things personally. At the slightest offense or disappointment, I'd feel personally attacked. Just straight-up triggered. I'd experience such a dip in my vibration that my body would respond with an instant stomachache that could last for days. And if that weren't enough, I'd experience brain fatigue—I just couldn't function right at all. It would wipe me out!

But when I gained vibrational awareness, the game changed. I was able to (1) stop being so easily triggered, (2) not take things personally, and (3) hold my vibration. Basically, I was able to vibrate higher and take my power back. I've come a mighty long way here. Lord knows.

These days, various types of disappointments no longer produce the same effect and reaction in my mind, body, vibration, and nervous system. They're no longer triggers. Offenses and disappointments no longer have control; they no longer have permission to lower my vibration and consume me to the point of disempowerment and impairment.

This is what vibrating higher daily can do. It shifts your mindset, elevates your perception, and neutralizes your triggers. Our higher vibration works like a shield—how empowering is that?! And while situations may still arise and cause me discomfort or stickiness, I don't stay down like I used to; the shield helps me return to my center and regain my power much more quickly.

Vibrating higher daily is how you win.

Your body's response to stimuli
is through your vibration.
Always pay attention to what your
vibration is communicating to you.

Effect on the Body

Vibration directly affects the body's biological processes, and therefore your quality of life. Healthy and high vibrations help maintain the internal energy of the body and its ability to self-regulate. Research has discovered that the body heals and repairs itself when it's vibrating at a certain rate and frequency. Early on, Royal Raymond Rife claimed in the 1930s that diseased cells vibrate and heal at certain frequencies. The late pioneer Dr. Valerie Hunt, professor emeritus of physiological science at UCLA, extensively studied human energy fields; and Dr. Bruce Lipton has explored the science of epigenetics and how our environment affects the cells in our bodies, maintaining that vibrations can alter our health and our biology.

Dr. Hunt performed many experiments on human energy fields and vibrations in food. For instance, in a video from 1986, she showed how a person eating junk food radiated a "dull and small" energy because the foods being eaten were "lifeless," "inert," and "dead" in vibration. Another person was filmed eating whole foods such as fruits, vegetables, grains, and seeds, and that person radiated an "enlivened" vibration because of the higher electromagnetic energies received from the food.

Would you love to vibrate higher and not feel dull? Eat healthy foods! A sign at the natural market where I shop stated that (wait for it) *only 9 percent* of adults eat their daily fruits and vegetables. Nine percent! We have to do better, people! Start seeing healthy foods as vibrational energy with superpowers. Because that's what they are.

Musicians have also found healing benefits of certain vibrations. For instance, musician, mystic, and healer Inayat Khan, who helped introduce Sufism to the West in the early twentieth century, recognized the importance and impact that music has on our vibrational frequency; as has contemporary musician Stephen Halpern, who also explores the healing properties of music and sound on the human mind, body, soul, and vibrational field.

The Impact That Vibes Have on Us

Your thoughts have an effect on your hormones. When you're feeling the vibration of love, your brain produces oxytocin. When you're happy, you produce serotonin. When you're feeling pleasure and gratification, dopamine. When you feel the vibration of fear or stress, and your fight-or-flight response kicks in, cortisol levels spike. All of these chemicals affect the body's well-being in various ways. Your body is paying close attention to your vibration and your thoughts.

Early on my path of becoming aware of how vibrational awareness can impact my physical body, I was able to combat and heal a life-threatening physical illness with alternative plant medicine and herbs.

It's said in some spiritual and healing traditions that "our issues are in our tissues" until we release them—meaning, people can carry their burdens, pain, and limited thinking in their bodies. Medical science has shown this. We have a different look and energy when we're worn down and defeated by life versus when we're overcoming and thriving in it. I give one answer when I'm asked my secret for looking so "youthful" or "radiant" at my age: "I vibrate higher daily." When we honor and nurture our vibration, our body rewards us by vibrating higher in health, well-being, and even radiant physical appearance. That's the best beauty secret I've found. But I did not always know this, or live by it.

What's more, the vibration of your thoughts governs your body's expressions, facial muscles, and reactions. When you become angry, you frown or furrow your brow; when happy, you smile or laugh; when charmed, you blush; when excited or frightened, your heart rate increases; when nervous or anxious, your stomach may ache; when stressed, your chest and breath may tense up; and when sad and distressed, your body produces tears. Your body is continually responding to the vibration of your thoughts and emotions. Thoughts create physical actions and responses in the body.

Your vibration, and the vibration of what you consume, creates an energy field that affects your health, consciousness, outer experiences, and overall state of being. This was the case with my overstimulated nervous system as a child, my health crises in my twenties, and eventually my healing journey through vibrational-based living.

SOUL
WORK

What I've learned, and relearn so very often, is this: certain things in our daily lives support us, heal us, and open our lives up in a whole new way. These things nurture the seeds of transformation within and help them to germinate, take root, and grow. To make this happen, make a pact with yourself to recognize and seek out what nourishes, nurtures, restores, and inspires you. When you make this pact, you move beyond a mentality of "things happen to me, and then I react" and into one of "things happen around me, and then I respond on my own (higher) terms."

The outside environment is always going to be there, and it's beyond your control, but you can choose what you give your attention and power to and how you respond.

Some people realize the power of vibration and respond in ways that affect the world positively, and some respond in ways that affect the world negatively and destructively. On the one side you have the peacemakers, heroes, and positive-change agents; on the other, you have those who cause chaos, dis-ease, distraction, and harm for their own gain and at the expense of everyone else. Low vibrational stimuli are so woven into our society and culture that they're nearly invisible. And as a human race, we've become more and more desensitized to them.

Many people don't question the "norm." But vibrating higher daily will mean questioning such things as the quality of the education system, the entertainment industry, social media, the food system, and all the things that influence society—and you—every day. Raising the vibration of who and what influences society brings about a better world for all. This could look like cultural progress among all races, societal healing, healthier options for all people, and more peace and higher purpose operating in the world. This is soul work.

Your Consent

You have not given consent to so much of what is influencing you (negatively) in the world, and surely to what is harming your health, and yet the influence and harm are happening. In my opinion, this is as uncool and not okay as it gets. This is vibrational violation. A silent dissonance allows this to be so and continue. But this can, and is, changing—especially through paths such as vibrational awareness and vibrational-based living.

Know that you can give consent to yourself. Allow yourself to be happier. To create boundaries. To say "no." To spend time the way you choose. To decide what holds your attention. To do what makes you vibrate higher and feel like yourself again.

If it lowers your vibration
it's not for you.
That's how you'll know.
If it raises your vibration
it's for you.
That's how you'll know.
Vibrations are guidance.

Pay attention to your vibration and internal cues. Stay mindful of how your vibration is responding to stimuli.

Healing Your Words and Thoughts

Your thoughts are an accumulation of your experiences. Make sure they're serving you well.

The overall state of your well-being, health, and vibration begins with a mindset. Your mindset is your mind's habits, your approach to situations and relationships, a process or belief, your mood, your inner nature, your self-talk, and your overall outlook on life. The vibration of your thoughts is governing your life, so make a pledge to yourself to use nourishing, supportive, and healing thinking.

A quick way to begin vibrating higher and shifting your life is to start practicing the art of replacing negative thoughts with positive ones. Think of when you listen to a radio, stream online, or watch TV: you change the channel or what's on-screen if it isn't for you. The mind works the same way: change the channel or screen as necessary. On a physiological level, replacing negative thoughts with positive ones rewires your brain and fires new neurons, which helps you sustain long-term success through elevating your thoughts and words.

You'll see. Take each disagreeable thought and rephrase it in a more positive, affirming, and agreeable way. If your thought is "I can't do this," replace it with "I'm more than capable and empowered to do this." Rephrase your thoughts and words in a way that serves you, rather than harms, hinders, or blocks you. We move toward what we speak. Consistency in how you speak and think is key so that you're not caught in a cycle of mental limbo and an

Keep taking control
and time for yourself,
until you're *you* again.

energetic tug-of-war between your desires, words, and thoughts. Use your thoughts and words as vehicles for your higher good—to elevate you, to free you, to advance you in life, and to guide you higher and higher.

Awareness in Tough Times

When you experience a trauma or life experience that brings you to your knees, you can deny, defend, or justify the wrongs, or blame, give up, or give in—or you can vibrate higher. Although negative responses may be gratifying on some level, lasting change and remedy don't come through these lower vibrations.

Vibrational awareness in tough times allows you to not continue on a path that's not serving your higher good—one that's keeping you in bondage and low vibrational cycles. Vibrational awareness enables you to seek higher ground and to use what happens to you as fuel for positive experiences, instead of being disempowered by what happens to you. And it also allows you to move beyond events—to being an overcomer and hero of your life.

Feeling like my life was out of my hands, I gave too much of my power, time, energy, and focus away to negative situations and people who meant me no good. I was living in a victim's mindset back then and had no real awareness of how to assert myself and insert myself into the world to make a better reality, have better experiences, and attract better people.

Your soul is requiring you
to enter the process and
journey: fully.

Your soul has guided you
here—now,

to growing, breaking
wide open,

and expanding.

All in order, to thrive and
vibrate higher daily.

Embody your healing
and power.

The moment you allow
what happened to
strengthen you, you win.

A Higher Power to Guide You

As you continue on your journey, or set off on it, remember that you are not alone. There's a Higher Power, a higher intelligence and plan at work. As you liberate yourself, rise above, and vibrate higher daily, you support the efforts of that Higher Power, you align with it, and you help it help you.

CONTEMPLATION

Choose What You Nurture + Nourish

All of life is here to be nurtured and nourished. In association with vibrational transformation, turn to some of the other universal pathways of restoration: meditation, natural or integrative medicine, spiritual rebirth, deep self-care, or shifting the atmosphere within yourself, your life, or your home. Consider how you can make such practices and pathways a personalized prescription to nourish yourself. What universal pathways work for you? What's your unique and personal path? If you don't yet know what helps you to feel mentally, physically, spiritually, creatively, and vibrationally nurtured and nourished, explore it. Explore how you best connect to the ultimate and sacred source of nurture and nourishment.

103

It's the quiet mind that gets
things done. . . .
When your conscious mind
is quiet and receptive,
the wisdom of your
subconscious rises to the
surface mind and you
receive your solution.

—JOSEPH MURPHY,
*Maximize Your Potential Through
the Power of Your Subconscious
Mind to Create Wealth and Success*

As you discover your pathways, find a way to return daily, or as often as possible, to gather higher vibrations, balance, and strength. Connecting to what makes you vibrate higher and feel like yourself again is the way toward living your power.

Take Time

Take time each day to fortify and recharge by connecting to what makes you vibrate higher. Do more of the things that affect you in a way that there's no language for—only feelings of vibrating higher. Keep in mind that the path for you may change during various seasons, terrains, and weather. Stay open, connected within, and in flow with your life and what best serves it and any given point on the path.

Harmonize

When you don't feel like yourself or you become overwhelmed by the journey, harmonize. This form of vibrational work is how you take your power back. It's stopping to put yourself back together. It's the gathering of yourself, your life, and your energy. It's finding a resting place. It's restoring your inner light. It's reclaiming your way. It's celebrating—or mourning—what you need to. It's releasing what doesn't belong to you and shedding what doesn't serve you. It's discharging and recharging. It helps nurture you into your wholeness.

It's sacred space you enter into and don't leave until you're fortified, vibrating higher, and feeling like yourself again.

Discharge the Energy

Because we are magnetic and energetic beings, vibrational influences in the world directly affect our vibrational wellness. We have to have a way of discharging the energy we accumulate in our everyday lives. This is crucial to maintaining a state of equilibrium, inner strength, and vibrational well-being. Vibrating higher daily is how we purify our lives of any unwanted outside influences. Take time to discharge.

Honor the Process

A sacred process is involved in getting you where you desire to be on your journey. Certain parts of the process cannot be skipped and are vital to the alignment of all the other parts. Take time to honor the entire process, including your mind, body, heart, spirit, soul, and lifestyle.

We honor the process by taking the necessary time to open up to it and allow change to come in. Just as vital, we honor the process by taking intentional action when we need to—even through fear, discomfort, and doubt. This in turn moves the process farther along and into higher levels.

Create Mood Awareness

Moods are vibes. They are our vibrations expressing themselves. They create the atmosphere and energy field around us and within us. Our moods highlight and reveal our current vibration. Our moods set the tone of our days and experiences. They are the way we express our vibration to the world.

Moods can be contagious and set the vibrational atmosphere of the spaces we enter and live in. Our most dominant and consistent mood eventually evolves into the vibrational theme of our days, weeks, months, years, life, and reality. We can experience many moods within the course of a day; it's up to us to decide which ones we allow and give power to.

Cultivate an Inner + Outer Sanctuary

We all need to have a place that's sacred and just for us, within and without. Create and give this space to yourself, over and over, however you can.

Turn to Self-Care

Self-care has profound healing abilities. It nourishes your mind, body, heart, and soul. It restores emotional, psychological, and spiritual harmony.

There were times where I was lost, hurting, exhausted, and looking for anyone who seemed to know how to help me find peace and healing. But then I discovered that through self-care, I had the power to shift my vibration within, so I no longer looked to other people to "fix" me. I remembered who I was, and I changed the game. Let's give it up for self-care and empowerment!

Keep liberating
yourself, until you're the
empowered *you* again.

3

A friend is someone who:

- invests in your healing
- gives you space to work on your vision and goals
- pauses to check in on you
- asks how they can best support you
- calls you out on your *mess*
- genuinely celebrates your progress

Trees, plants, flowers, herbs, minerals, air, and water—all possess a greater purpose for being here. Each is part of a greater thing constantly happening for the greater good of all beings—nourishing, sustaining, and helping other beings outside of themselves to thrive and grow.

We were created with the same potential to sustain and maintain life for others outside of ourselves. We're a part of this same ongoing, ever-present, and always

OTHERS

working ecosystem in unseen ways that are so subtle that we cannot feel or recognize them. But there are countless other ways that are very seen, obvious, felt, and clear to us. We humans are part of one big ecosystem; we are having a symbiotic experience with one another, throughout our life and times here on earth—no getting around it or escaping it. It's happening.

And vibrating higher daily and living your power is how you thrive in the midst of it all.

THE RIGHT PEOPLE OVER THE WRONG PEOPLE

Throughout my journey, I've realized that often, my greatest joys and greatest pains come from other people. I'm not alone: the most common questions I get from fellow students of life revolve around relationships with others.

In the field of chemistry, we know that certain things do and don't mix well together. Certain things combined become toxic matter, while other things combined become supportive tonics and remedies—higher functioning matter. People, opportunities, and relationships work this way too.

My usage of the words *the wrong people* does not mean that the people themselves are wrong, but that the way they interact with you chemically and vibrationally impacts you—your soul, your goals, your journey, and your health and well-being—in a negative way. They're not compatible with you. In chemistry, what's wrong for one element or compound can be right for another. So it's all

The right people bring

your soul medicine.

about observing and knowing the right and wrong mixture of matter and energies in your life's laboratory. And at times on your journey you'll find that what may be right for one person, may not be right and best for you.

You are the chemist of your life, and through vibrational awareness, you can become more empowered, even masterful, in this role. How you combine people and opportunities with your life can be done with higher purpose, skill, and benefit to your higher good. You distinguish between what's for you and what's not for you with greater accuracy, even speed.

The Problem with Letting the Wrong People In

After I'd left the abusive relationship in my twenties, I thought I had moved on from the wrong people. But what often happens to victims of abuse was happening to me: I left the abusive relationship, but I still hadn't left the mindset created by the relationship or by the unresolved spiritual wounds that had gotten me there in the first place. As a victim of traumatic circumstances, I fell into the spectrum of those who spiral downward after their experiences with trauma, and in time I lost my way even more.

My wounds were still fresh and exposed, and the person who showed up next in my life saw me in my weakened vibrational state and took advantage of me. Instead of being protected or rescued, as I so yearned to be, I was abused and taken advantage of all the more. My suicide attempt was partly because of the presence of this wrong relationship in my life.

I've shared this part of my story publicly and learned that I'm not alone. We are not alone. Being around people who hurt us and don't serve us—from toxic friends to dysfunctional family members to emotionally or physically abusive partners—has consequences, but we can forgive ourselves, forgive them (because holding unforgiveness can turn into an inner energetic toxin), and move on with better people, toward a better life, in peace and harmony.

Many of us have some aspect of our story we desire to improve, to edit, to transcend, or to redeem ourselves from. Maybe it's still a tender area for you to touch and work on. It was for me—for years. But I've learned that on some level, we're all putting thought to rising above our old narratives, to reconfiguring our lives. Even when we don't realize it, healing is a unifying and liberating thing. What I thought were only wasted years in my early twenties—letting the wrong people in, being involved in the wrong things, and feeling lost, confused, misguided, and depressed—turned out to be defining years.

My mindset at the time, reminiscent of South Central LA street culture, was this: do whatever you have to do to survive. A side hustle here and there, toxic friends here and there, and a lost path all came with the territory. Looking back, the pattern of creating social connections around pain, survival, and dysfunction, instead of higher vibrations, was a low vibrational cycle for me.

Out of desperation,
boredom, or loneliness, you
can be tempted to entertain
the wrong relationships.
Remember your goals,
and rise above.

Forgive yourself for
all of the relationships
and friendships you settled
for when you weren't in
your power.

I send my younger self so much love. Bless her heart. At that time, she was lost and in much need of higher awareness, vibrations, and guidance, which would eventually, through divine intervention, show up. She let the wrong people in only because she, like many of us, felt alone and misunderstood, and she was not in her power. She didn't have the right people in her life, and that's a feeling that many of us share. We all desire to have the right people, the right friends and relationships, in our lives.

Wherever you are, you are not alone, dear one. Lots of self-love, self-forgiveness, inner power, and grace. And along with that, humor. Remember, finding the humor in it all is soul cleansing. Laughter is healing.

This intentional way of living will help you make choices with a lighter heart and with more clarity. It also makes it easier to respect your boundaries and your higher good.

The Wrong People

- Make you compromise your truth and higher good
- Are repeatedly unreliable and inconsiderate
- Don't check in on you
- Downplay your opinions, feelings, ideas, and good news
- Don't want to see you grow and rise above, and instead keep you stuck in negative cycles with them

- Can reverse your progress and self-care
- Don't respect your boundaries
- Don't work on their inner lives in any progressive, productive, or deliberate way
- Don't grow with you in a harmonious way
- Don't reciprocate the energy, support, and love you give
- Don't live with integrity
- Discourage and distract you from vibrating higher and living in your power

With work and transformation, I no longer put myself in situations where I compromise my boundaries, truth, power, or authentic feelings. These days, I sustain my soul's integrity, with delight and with way more composure and ease. The more you live your power, the stronger a force you become in your life. How divine!

The right relationships are like pieces to the puzzle of our life. They fit in just the right place, as only they can. The contrast between the right relationships and the wrong ones can and should make us acknowledge and appreciate all the more any and all of the great and healthy people and relationships in our lives.

Have Patience: Sometimes the Right People Take Time

Though many of the right people enter our lives seamlessly, some take time. Some relationships need adjustment to make them fit our

High vibrational
relationships are about
attracting the people
you're on the same higher,
healthy, and supportive
wavelength with. They're
about higher alignment,
harmony, and purpose.

You can always shift and transform from being the antagonist or toxic one into being the high vibrational, harmonious one. Think *reconfiguration*.

life puzzle, or chemistry. The best and right relationships survive this process. The ones that we try to force to fit often end up hurting, unfulfilling, or disappointing us. These are friendships and relationships we must let go of: your highest good is to move on and beyond, keeping in mind that you're a chemist at work. And as Don Miguel Ruiz teaches in his book *The Four Agreements*, we can choose not to "personalize" the outcome. Remember—it's all chemistry, it's not personal. Whew! How freeing is that?

My sweet mother was one of those people who took time to be a healthy presence in my life. My younger years with her were rocky and hard to journey through at times, but I kept on loving her, as did my siblings, and as she did us. During her troubled fourth marriage I was always waiting for her to heal and to come to her full senses so she could love me right, be more emotionally present, and be who and what I needed her to be as a mother. By the grace of The Divine, that day would indeed come. She finally vibrated out of the marriage that wasn't serving her. She rose above, into her power, and she let the toxic relationship go. And it wasn't until after that last divorce—which was her dark night of the soul—that she got it. She transformed and reconfigured herself, and she became the mother I had been longing for. For the rest of her life, she lived happily single and became the sweet, endearing, and soul-nourishing grandmother and mother of our dreams. She took her power back. She reconfigured. She vibrated higher and inspired us all.

Life is complicated. People are complicated. Sometimes relationships take time to become beautiful and functional, and at other times they simply never blossom or function right. At all. If a shoe doesn't fit, you naturally move on to find one that does. The right relationships and friendships are like that. Don't force the wrong things to fit. And certainly don't mix things together that shouldn't be mixed. It's all about . . . say it loud and unapologetically with me: chemistry!

Keep in mind that as the chemist of your life, your laboratory is your home, your health, your goals, your environment, and your relationships.

The Right People

Having the right people around you builds you up and creates a sustainable and harmonious environment, which adds extra goodness to your life.

I made it through the most difficult terrains of my journey with the support of the right people. I felt then, as I do today, grateful to be valued, seen, heard, nurtured, safely held in community, and loved by these people. When I was most broken and lost, it was others who helped me pull my heart and life back together—no matter whether I asked for it or not. In my tender and fragile moments, they hugged me, softly caressed my back, or conversed with a comforting tone. Without judgment, they stayed with me on some of my most perplexing, wearying, and frustrating days. Amid unharmonious vibrations from within or without, they helped me to find my note and reharmonize my life and mind.

My friendship goals and intentions are to return the love, to make sure that I reciprocate the soulful giving that is offered to me. This balance matters to me. It's important that others feel in return the support and love they give me. Everybody wins when a relationship is in harmony and balance.

I'm on my way. These four words let you know it's real. When my heart was in pieces in the summer of 2018 as my mother lay in a coma before me, on the verge of death, one of my best friends, Devine, immediately responded with these words.

He was on tour, many hours and states away from us, and he found his way across all of those states and hours to come and sit by my side in the hospital and help hold my broken heart together. His working out whatever was necessary to leave the tour, book a flight, track down a rental car, and show up with food and blankets, all at the midnight hour, was nothing but The Most High moving through him. Devine stayed right by my and my siblings' side while my mother was still with us in the hospital's Palliative Care Unit to a couple of days after her homegoing, which he spoke so beautifully and movingly at. *He brought my soul medicine.* This is high vibrational friendship.

But the right people aren't just the ones who make dramatic gestures to help us put our lives back together. Sometimes they are simply fun and joyful presences in our lives. The right people can remind us that comedy can be found in the serious, mundane, and stressful moments too. A good laugh has untriggered me on many

Maybe a
better word for
relationships is
nurture-ships.

occasions—and brought me back to myself. As Dr. Seuss says to us all, "Funny things are everywhere." Thank The Divine for the people who help us find them!

Whenever we can't do it for ourselves, other people show up with a life raft, a tow truck, a joke, or at times a sharp sword to help untangle us, set us free, and save us somewhere on our journey.

Some people become your friend from a higher place. They organically come closer to your heart and soul than most. You feel this closeness profoundly. And it feels like coming home, every time. Not every relationship has to be like this, but to have this, or to be this for another soul, is like journeying with an angel.

Looking through a spiritual lens, I realize where my help comes from. The Divine was, and is, the current moving through this person, and that person, in our lives, at such times.

The Right People

- Naturally bring your soul medicine
- Listen and sincerely lean toward you in supportive ways
- Give you the sweet or hard truth, or both, when necessary
- Are reliable and considerate
- Check in on you
- Inspire and positively challenge you out of your comfort zone
- Respect your boundaries

- Grow and vibrate higher with you
- Work on their inner lives in progressive, productive, or mindful ways
- Don't downplay your opinions, feelings, ideas, or good news
- Genuinely celebrate your success and progress
- Reinforce your need for self-care
- Reciprocate the energy, support, and love you give
- Live in integrity
- Encourage you to vibrate higher and live your power

THE HELPER +
THE ASSIGNMENT

Our relationships are a two-way street: just as we find ourselves comforted by others, we also help those we care about.

We are sent. We become deployed to the front lines during times of need as conduits, vessels, soldiers, and earth angels. This happens through a call to action, a sense of higher purpose, or, if we hesitate, a spiritual shove forward into action. Maybe it's to check on someone; to respond in a helpful way; to prepare and deliver a meal; to do the right thing; to do what seems like a random act of kindness or love or a good deed; to show up, serve, and spend time in someone's process with them; to communicate certain words or a message—on and on. So many ways the orders come through, and to, us.

For the current to come through, however, we have to stay open to it in our heart. And when we do, we become vessels and conduits on earth, or "helpers," as Fred Rogers, of *Mister Rogers' Neighborhood*, calls them.

When we help others, we also help ourselves. And it's so often an essential part of our own spiritual wellness and growth during whatever current season of life we're in or journeying toward. Often, an assignment received that seemingly has nothing to do with us and our journey has everything to do with us and our journey. It's connected, and we're meant to be involved.

Living in vibrational awareness has a way of opening us up and keeping us available as conduits in this way. And as Mother Teresa, by way of Saint Teresa of Avila's prayer, would so often pray, it allows us to be The Divine's hands and ears here on earth. Even during times of busyness, inconvenience, or our own times of need, we are still on call.

Discernment + Wisdom

Not every circumstance or potential relationship will be your assignment. Dealing in the multidimensional realm of relationships is a spiritual art, and it takes wisdom to maneuver with purpose, and in wellness and wholeness and in your power. Discerning the difference between who needs your help and who does not is vital because who we serve contributes to our own vibration, spiritual wellness, and growth process.

You can discern your assignment when you're coming from a place of pure love and empowerment, and when there's no threat to you becoming disempowered. Disempowerment looks like vibrating in a lower state, losing your harmony, and being repeatedly taken advantage of, manipulated into action, or spiritually weakened as a result of an unhealthy relationship.

You'll also recognize it's not your assignment or relationship when your motivation is coming from a self-centered, egoic state of mind. Ulterior motives are never a higher call to action. In times like these, simply breathe out ego, breathe in higher wisdom, and chill. And know that only what you do in high vibrations will truly last, count, and remain standing. Everything else is a fading mist that you can't hold on to or a dream from which you'll have to wake up at some point to return to life and reality.

Connect to the Love

When you feel most alone on your journey, when you're in the desert, tap into the wondrous resources within. Reflect on the ways others have shown up for you in the past. And realize that you come from a village, no matter how big or small. Even though you may be away from it at times, or your tribe members are no longer with you in the physical realm, you're still a part of the village. You're part of the whole. Connect to your energy bond and the place within your heart and soul where the love you experienced and felt is stored. The love you're missing is right there within you, accompanying you on your journey, awaiting your recognition. It lies low, in reserve, until you give it permission to take up more space in your life.

Love is about coming together. Souls are whole alone, but when they come together for a unified purpose, they become whole in a different and more extraordinary way. That's the power of coming together with other beings.

And whether positive or negative, connection amplifies the spirit of what's there. What's there sets the tone for the relationship, for the community, and for the space, which directly influences spirit, experiences, purpose, and vibration.

The right assignments and
relationships keep you on
the right track. The wrong
relationships distract.
That's how you'll know.

When you're not feeling
like yourself
and you're burdened
by life and the journey,
lean on a loved one to help
lighten the load.

Taking the Path of Growth Together

One of my great longtime friends is filmmaker and writer Christopher Erskin. He was there during each of my low vibrational relationships and way before them all.

With laughter in my soul, I recall calling him up once after not being in touch for a while. I said something super simple like, "Hi, Christopher, apologies it's taken me so long to make this call to you." And he responded just like this: "Who is he? Are you okay? What did he do to you? Do I need to come and get you? I can leave now. Where are you?"

Goodness! While grateful for his inner gangster jumping to my rescue, I had to tell brother man to stand down. I laughed so loud from my soul. Comedy! He didn't know my life update. I had come a long way since we'd last spoken, and I filled him in. I let him know the details of my healing and growth, and it felt glorious to not be "that Lalah" anymore. This time, I was calling from a position of empowerment.

When you've been friends with someone a long time, you see that person grow. It's magnificent to see your beloved friends, family, or companions living out their healing and transformation, and for them to see you doing the same. It's an energy cleanse of the relationship and its environment, and it also raises the vibration of the connection. Growth is a beautiful thing to behold and is what life is all about. So if you aspire to value, maintain, sustain, and elevate your relationships to their highest potential and purpose, grow together.

My conversations with friends nowadays, including Christopher, have shifted from disempowered and low vibrational narratives to life goals. They are about purpose instead of rescue and survival. They celebrate inspiration and progress instead of rehashing cycles of repeated relationship problems. This is a true glow up that took effort, time, and growth on all of our parts, during which any person or relationship that wasn't growing was organically outgrown and succeeded by a better, more harmonious one.

Pruning

Human relationships are like the root systems and branches of trees—they're extensions of us. When we care for trees, we have to prune dead limbs and leaves in order to make space for the appropriate environment for growth, fruitfulness, and thriving to occur. No longer having to deal with the various side effects of the dead or decaying limbs and leaves attached to it, the tree now has more energy to focus on growth, fruitfulness, and thriving. We reflect nature in this same way. Feel familiar to you?

This process is what makes trees and gardens—and people—beautiful. We notice the integrity, love, nurturing, and energy that someone puts into a good pruned area or life. We notice the level of care, intention, and soulful grooming that makes way for greater growth and development. This allows us to experience a sense of harmony and beautiful vibrations as a result. This is how we can feel better after being in certain gardens and around certain people.

Healthy lives and relationships don't just happen; they take work, nurturing, and pruning. What isn't working or growing? What needs to be trimmed away or dug up from the roots? What is negatively affecting the whole and spreading like a virus?

Notice the decaying or affected parts. Notice what's already died off. Notice the people who aren't contributing to your life in a supportive or positive way. Who without regard for your well-being or process, are the people who have settled into the role of being a subtle nuisance, or an outright antagonist, in your life and to your process. They can show up in big, small, or subtle ways, but always with the same destructive and low vibrational goal in mind.

The right people help you to grow and maintain a thriving and beautiful tree of life. That's how you'll know who they are. By knowing how to prune your own life, and by valuing and honoring the process, you grow more able to show up as a better friend, beloved, and support in the lives of other people. Making space in your life for great people to be in it—true friends, mentors, supportive family, spiritual community—builds you up and gives you an extra layer of protection, nourishment, and guidance. All part of maintaining your healthy tree of life.

As part of my healing journey, and as homework from my mentors, I began making space in the garden of my life for only those

How you journey and treat
people is your vibration.
How people journey and
treat you is theirs.

who were also focused on growth and thriving. Honoring this process and boundary has allowed for a more productive, rewarding, and fulfilling journey since. This was the gateway for me to experience enriching relationships all around.

I've learned that letting go is not a rude thing or a personal thing—it's a spiritual and purposeful thing. It's about knowing and honoring that you're here to be the good caretaker of the garden within you, and of all the fruit you're here to bear.

Honoring the Process of Letting Go

Some relationships never ascend to higher heights or fulfill their intended purpose. There's too much negative weight or lack of motivation to go higher, and so the whole "ship" remains stuck in place, in lower vibrations. It maybe even sinks. And what could have been great for all involved never reaches a functional place. It never fully sets sail.

How many times have you tried sailing a relation-"ship" that was too heavy, or not adequate for the journey ahead, and it capsized and sank? When the whole thing starts sinking, don't sink with it! It's up to you to jump ship and save yourself!

In these moments of letting go, vibrational awareness allows you to remember and honor your appointed work and destination in life and to eventually choose people who are traveling the same way. Heal, grow, and rise above together!—that whole glorious thing!

It all comes down to our not holding space for the pain to linger longer than it should. Pain has its place in healing and growth, but it should never be a destination where we take up permanent residence. With grace, it's about making sure to get back to where we belong, our place of empowerment.

Letting go of relationships can and should be done from a place of vibrational integrity. As you vibrate out of connections that don't serve you, a huge part of your empowerment is vibrating higher while you're exiting. Keep in mind that the goal is to vibrate higher, even when it hurts and is triggering. And reaching that level of spiritual and vibrational kung fu takes work. But be assured, it's an empowering and freeing posture once you're there. Don't allow yourself to get caught up in any vibrational ego wars with other people. Compose yourself, refocus, and let go.

Who Is in Your Mirror?

Your life will mirror back to you your closest friends, so choose people who are a beautiful reflection of how you desire your life to be. What's in the mirror? Growth, empowerment, and thriving? I knew I was in the right friendships when I looked around and everyone was thriving.

When I think of my mirror, two of the primary people who come to mind are my Uncle Willie, one of the seven African American World War II heroes honored in 2018 by Congresswoman Maxine Waters, and my Aunt Helen, a retired registered nurse. They are both in their nineties now and are still thriving and as lively as ever. I grew up very close to them from childhood and even stayed with Uncle Willie and Aunt Helen for a while during my lost years right

No longer responding
or reacting to people
who trigger you
is one of the best ways
to strengthen your
spiritual muscles.

You journey differently with
the right people in your life.
The right people understand
you and nourish you from a
whole other level.

after high school. They took me in, nurtured me, and displayed nothing but pure old-fashioned love.

Uncle Willie still calls me Shuga as a term of endearment, as he's done for as long as I can remember, and ends our conversations by saying, "You take care of yourself. You know the way home." These genuine words move my heart and nourish my soul every time I hear them. Feeling held and looked after in a rich way by my oldest living relatives in this modern, fast digital age is medicinal and sacred, and I cherish it so very much.

Conversations in the right relationships are full of balance, encouragement, and inspiration. In these relationships, if we do talk about heavy situations or feelings of disempowerment, it's not just for the sake of it, or to stay there and put a period on it; it's to work together toward transformation and progress. Together, we pivot and vibrate higher. These relationships are refreshingly solution-oriented. The wrong relationships, in contrast, are only focused on the problem. And in that case, Lalah has left the chat!

Where in your life can you observe problem-centered relationships? Be mindful of these flags in other people:

- They find only fault in themselves, you, and others.
- They always share bad news.
- They speak down to, belittle, or dishonor you and others.
- They don't honor your needs or requests for a more positive connection and environment.

The best relationships
energetically leave
a light on for you
and warmly
welcome you in.

- They focus on what triggers you, rather than on what empowers and settles you.
- They aren't interested in resolving problems in the long term.
- Because of their own inner settings, progress is short-lived and scarce for them.
- They prefer to remain in toxic situations and expect you to joyfully visit them there.

If you find yourself with friends like these, please know that they are not friends at all. Somebody had to tell you.

Vibrational-based living is about stepping into your power—in this case, the power to decide who to allow into your life.

THE RELATIONSHIP WITH YOURSELF: THE HERO OF YOUR LIFE

We often expect others to be the remedy, or the hero. This is nice in fairy tales and books, but in real life (music stops with record scratch sound effect here, please), *you*, sweet beloved soul, are the hero. Whenever you feel heavily ladened or like the underdog, remember that. Just as Dorothy in *The Wiz*, played by Diana Ross, and in *The Wizard of Oz*, played by Judy Garland, discovers in the end, you have the power all along.

If I were to give you homework for self-worth, it would be to watch *The Wiz* with the original cast and meditate on the song "If You Believe," sung by Lena Horne in the movie and by Diana Ross on the soundtrack. Both versions of this song are spirituals in my opinion. Watch the film and see yourself as each of the characters: Dorothy, rising to her place of empowerment in the world; Scarecrow, gaining wisdom; the Tin Man, gaining a heart; and the Cowardly Lion, gaining courage. The journey down the yellow brick road is a metaphor that we can each insert ourselves into at different terrains, seasons, and junctions of life. Watch the movie with Joseph Campbell's hero motif in mind, with the dark night of the soul in mind, and with this book's metaphorical terrains in mind.

Your mindset can send you into further distress, anxiety, and disempowerment around others, or it can awaken and activate the warrior and hero within to rise and turn all the way up: as much as necessary. Be wary of which mindset you are enabling. Implementing the practices within this book will support your inner hero and your mission, and keep you fortified on the journey.

In dire times, you may be the only one available to *you*. Knowing this has allowed me to vibrate higher and be okay with or without anyone else in sight. Here are two strategies I use for checking in on my relationship with myself.

Strength also looks like
opening up and asking
for help from friends,
family, spiritual
community, and mentors
when necessary,
and awakening the
hero within
when no one sees your
beacon or shows up.

Like a Magnet

Self-worth is like a magnet. It affects so much of how others treat us, communicate with us, and relate to us. How are you taking your place in the world and among others? Are you living your power? Are you living in a healthy vibration of self-worth? Or are you living in a self-defeating state, mindset, and life?

A big part of self-worth is knowing and remembering who you are, even in the presence of others. It's one thing to feel empowered when you're alone in your personal sacred world, but it's another to live in your power and self-worth when you're out in the world relating to and dealing with others.

Change the Inner Narrative

Sometimes the disempowering conversations we have aloud with other people are actually reflections of the internal ones that we've had with ourselves for years. When we believe that it's acceptable to speak negatively to ourselves, we often allow others to speak poorly to us. Change how you speak to yourself internally, and you'll change everything.

Once I stopped having those harmful conversations with myself and instead spoke and honored more affirming ones, I saw myself differently, and better relationships and conversations showed up in my life.

When you love
yourself and know
your worth, what you
allow looks different.

VISUAL ___
EXERCISE

Draw a tree, and on each of its branches place the name of a person in your life. For the people who are in your life in a positive way, draw a big green leaf on that branch. For the people who are distracting you from thriving, who are not serving you in a positive way, and whose energy branch has died but is still attached to you, draw a red flag on that branch.

Seeing the red flags allows you to recognize what needs pruning from your life in order for your tree to grow more full, more fruitful, more beautiful, and more healthy. After you see what needs pruning, work on it. Do this exercise with vibrational awareness and nonjudgment. Pruning isn't a bad thing. Simply clip and move, then repeat, as in release from the tree of your life anyone who is a clear red flag. Graciously prune where necessary while living in your power. If you feel tender after trimming someone out of your tree, give the healing some time. Time closes and heals all wounds. And treasure the fact that by pruning your personal tree of life, you support and signal glorious new life to birth into existence.

Seize your power and
your rightful position in
the garden of life.

Follow your nudge to reach out to loved ones.
You never know how much you'll be a vessel
for The Divine and conduit to another soul.
When you seek approval from outside of
yourself, be mindful not to become solely
reliant on the gratifying validation of others.
Leaving it up to others to recognize what
I needed to recognize for myself caused
many unfulfilled relationships. While not
all had the potential to thrive, some did,
and maybe could have been more beautiful
had I been in my higher awareness.
So thank goodness for growth here.
At times, you'll have to pause and recognize
how far you've come and appreciate it
for yourself, regardless of whether
anyone else does—or doesn't.
Self-acknowledgment of your growth and
efforts is critical to remaining in your power.
It's how I took my power—and joy—
back many times.
Your own love is divine soul medicine.

4

You have come this far. You have become aware of energy and vibration in a new and more empowering way. You have journeyed through many terrains, and you have discovered the hero within. You have learned how to nurture the right relationships in your life and how to handle the not-so-great ones. You are doing the inner work. With this ever-growing and empowering awareness, a new invitation now emerges: turn your attention and intention *outward*.

It is no secret that the world we live in poses daily challenges. As your eyes and heart open to what's going on, the picture becomes clearer and clearer. There are endless ways in which systemic and vibrational hindrances overwhelm us and even hold us back. Information and education are unbalanced and have proved numerous times to be untrustworthy, irresponsible, and biased. The modern-day health food supply and industry are not accessible to all—being too expensive

The journeys you've been
through reconfigure how
you show up in the world.

for the majority of people who so urgently need healthy foods. Our televisions, newspapers, and social media flood us on psychological, heart, and soul levels with toxic messages of fear, hatred, separatism. It's hard to find nourishing, positive messages of hope, courage, love, peace, harmony, and progress when such stories are overshadowed and drowned out by all the toxicity.

More and more, mainstream culture is created and influenced by big-budget marketing instead of genuine and relatable voices. And what's more, our mind and bodies—from our nervous systems to our hormonal systems to our thought processes and behavioral patterns—have come under attack, often altered by toxic chemicals in medicine, water, and everyday household products. Many awakened experts and leaders in the fields of health, spirituality, and science have recognized this as modern-day chemical warfare.

Our response used to be to simply give in, give up, and tune out—until a much greater force began to shake us awake to take our power back. How do we show up in a world that we recognize as toxic, wounded, divided, and hurting in all directions while we are seeking enlightenment, healing, balance, harmony, and a higher vibrational life? And how do we exit the metaphorical terrains and the life we've overcome with higher perspective, power, and purpose?

TAKING YOUR PLACE IN THE WORLD

Many people remain desensitized to the low vibrations of our world, but *you* have now begun awakening and feeling and rising in self-compassion and compassion toward others. You are waking up, snapping out of a spell, and realizing which of the hypnotic, damaging ways of the world don't serve or benefit you. Like you, more and more people are collectively rising and growing into this vibrational awareness daily.

A vibrationally aware and empowered life serves not only you; it also serves the world around you. Self-care and personal development matter. They help us discover our own inner power, which is the only way we can thrive in the long term. Moreover, a Higher Power and plan are at work, taking our daily awareness of vibrational forces and radiating it outward. It's true alchemy. And as we vibrate higher daily, live our power, and show up as conduits, we support this divine good, ultimately nourishing and helping to reconcile the human and environmental conditions around us.

This state, one that is aligned with a purpose beyond ourselves,

The problem is
vibrational, and
the solution is
vibrational.

allows us to cease journeying with no real sense of direction or a clear place to go. We are in the driver's seat. We have a choice to honor and follow higher guidance and to not judge the outcome or work at hand solely on the basis of our own human ability, experience, limiting beliefs, or fears. Fear can become a major restraint on the journey.

Failure to Launch

Many of us from time to time, myself included, have found launching into the world in a greater way frightening, complex, and outright triggering. Especially when we're just coming home to ourselves. During this process, opening and expanding outward into the world is a lot to comprehend and fully digest. In response, we may run or hide from the call when we get it and may even find ourselves living in a state of rebellion and limbo. When this happens, we stay with what's familiar and comfortable, even when familiar and comfortable are not what's most nurturing, beneficial, and purposeful for our soul and its journey.

The phrase *failure to launch* refers to young people struggling with the transition of leaving their home base and entering into the adult world. But it can also symbolically represent something that happens spiritually and metaphorically among people of diverse ages and backgrounds. There are various reasons why we fail to launch out of our comfort zones. Maybe our gifts and talents were never acknowledged, developed, or supported, and so we have a hard time inserting ourselves into the world. Maybe we've been overnurtured or undernurtured or sheltered by a parent or caregiver, like a plant that gets too much or not enough water or is not placed in the right light. Or maybe we don't recognize when we've outgrown certain environments or relationships.

It's vital to our soul's growth to continually develop ourselves, and a key part of this experience is launching our lives outward, forward, and beyond. When we do so, a life of stagnation, resistance, or limbo is replaced with a life of movement, higher passion, and surrender to purpose. Inertia defeated!

Like Dorothy in *The Wizard of Oz* and *The Wiz*, we are journeying on our own yellow brick road in search of ourselves and overcoming various conditions and terrains along the way. Metaphorically, we too are in search of "home"—a nourishing home base from which we go forth and live our power in the world.

It takes power that we don't always think we have to do what we are called to do. Whenever I find myself feeling inadequate in the world of work and purpose, I remember that there's always a higher source of power within. Keeping close to what helps my faith stay alive, active, and strong keeps me on track. A nourishing home base for me is my spiritual life and relationship with The Divine, spending time with loving and nurturing souls, and doing the things that make me vibrate higher daily. What's home to you?

Expansion: Into the World You Go

As you move beyond an outgrown life, overcome fearfulness, shift from unharmonious cycles, or break self-destructive patterns, you enter the realm of greater purpose. You reconfigure yet again—this time, though, focused on self and the greater collective good. Here, an awakened drive and power come over you. No longer unwilling or afraid to take your place in the world, you set off to manifest and advance high vibrational living in expressive and effective ways. And as you continue moving through life deeply rooted in higher awareness of who you are, you're able to find your place of power in the movement and mission of life.

When I found myself on the path to vibrational awareness and eventually radiating that awareness outward, the things I did and the way I created shifted as a divine by-product of surrendering to my transformation and healing journey. My soul's goal and desire were now to do that which I felt called to do. But that didn't mean the path was without obstacles.

Going into the world with your gifts can be scary. When I decided to share with others my tips, advice, and insight on vibrational-based living, I started doing so for free via emails, phone calls, and online. Blocked by fear and self-doubt, I resisted turning what I loved and was told I was good at into a living. I often thought, *Am I qualified enough? Will I be taken seriously? Who will compensate me for this? Will I be judged? Will I succeed? Who am I to do this*

What makes you vibrate

higher is the way.

Doing *you* is a big
part of what heals and
empowers you.

anyway? These kinds of questions overpowered my mind. They kept me playing small and on the sidelines of life.

I began to look deeper to assess whether desiring to stay in my comfort zone was holding me back. And yep, indeed it was.

Realizing that my comfort zone had become a block—a low vibration of fear—I chose to rise above it by honoring my gifts and talents more. As numerous sacred texts teach us, knowing how to honor and use our gifts will make room for us in the world. Once I surrendered my gifts to The Divine's plan and began making steps in that direction, the path unfolded as I took each step. I've continued taking steps on the path daily. Hello, new way of being in the world, new reality, new me!

Launching into the world isn't just one step, of course. It's a process. An ongoing one. I remember being a bundle of nerves before my first speaking engagement, and my sister, who was living in another state at the time, jumped on a plane to be by my side. With her cheering me on, I was able to calm my nerves, and with a small amount of courage, I walked toward the podium and I gave my first public talk. And I survived it. Afterward, we celebrated with our favorite smoothies and great food. Cheers to doing your thing out there, self!

Years later, I found myself once again overcoming a similar obstacle in order to continue to expand my work in the world. I was launching my first-ever website, which was a milestone for my business, and the moment I was ready to hit the button and publish it, I paused.

All of the common self-doubts arose within me again. I said to my friend Devine and daughter, India, who were right by my side supporting me on launch night, that maybe I should wait another two days. This would give me plenty of time to work out the small issues that showed up at the last minute, I reasoned. All I can say is India and Devine are heaven sent, pun intended. Humorously, they both let me know *it was going to be a problem* if I didn't hit the publish button and launch myself into the world at 12:00 a.m. And so at midnight, I did it, I launched. Into the world I went.

Devine and India were my reinforcements. They helped me stay accountable, on task, courageous, and on course. And I recognized and honored the force working through them to help me.

What I've learned about launching into the world is that the power comes by doing the work and taking the necessary steps forward. Fear and resistance may show up, but through awareness, we recognize these feelings as the terrains they are and journey forward and beyond them with wisdom. The path becomes clearer by traveling it. The learning curves and failures along the way are gifts and part of our higher development and awakening as conduits. And allowing someone we trust to hold us accountable and keep us on purpose is paramount. These are your reinforcements. You will also meet and manifest the most amazing people who will help you along the way as you journey with purpose.

None of this—my supportive friendships, relationships, and work as a spiritual teacher—would have become my new reality had I remained trapped in doubts, fears, and limiting beliefs. I had to expand my awareness, intention, and efforts toward ultimately living my power in the world. No more fear-based living for me! Pattern interrupted!

Remember: vibrational-based living teaches us that all things are interconnected. The high vibrations that carried and lifted you and the low ones that brought you to your knees didn't happen without a greater purpose: everything is interwoven. And like the good sacred book says, all things work together for good when you're living in higher alignment and reverence. When you become a clear channel through which The Divine and high vibrations can flow and work, you can create real and undeniable change.

BECOME
A BEACON

As awakened beings, we are aware that everything we do is going to impact others; therefore it's necessary to be forces for good. We recognize the power of interconnectedness, and so with honor we serve the world with high intentions instead of low ones.

We each have a unique role to play in the combined solution to the pain, suffering, and imbalance in our world. More and more as you become a visible expression of vibrational awareness and harmony, the world meets you in a new way. Your new inner power becomes a gateway to outer change, and you become available in a greater way. You show up, respond, and contribute differently when your vibration and harmony are in a good place. And consequently, you become a beacon of inspiration and hope to others. Your vibration, being seen and felt, becomes a lighthouse in the world. In various ways, we each hold this much power and purpose. Reaching our higher empowerment is critical not only to our own personal journey, but to that of the collective world as well.

As we progress onward by living an intentional life through vibrational-based living and service, we show up in the world from a higher place of integrity and care. Fully immersing ourselves in this way of being allows us to transform even the most mundane days, tasks, and experiences into the extraordinary.

These extraordinary experiences happen in our homes, our work, our relationships, and our communities. Maybe you start making an effort to send a birthday or a "thinking of you" card to a friend. Perhaps you start volunteering with at-risk youth, serving at your child's school, or helping out at a library. Maybe you spread stomach-joy among colleagues by baking special treats to enjoy at the end of a long week. Or you try to strike up conversations with strangers. Or maybe you go big and more personal, such as opening your home to a friend in need.

A fulfilled life
is about living
in your higher
awareness,
power, and
purpose.

Unexpected opportunities of kindness
and healing are all around. Initiate them.

Sometimes a big spotlight shines on your good efforts and deeds; at other times the good you do is recognized by only one or two other souls; and at other times no one sees it other than The Divine. The work is sacred nonetheless, and you do what has to be done because it's the right thing to do. As someone who is aware of the ripple effect of vibrations, you know your good deeds have the potential to impact people in large and small necessary ways.

There are times when our individual work, strength, and capability can feel inadequate, but know that cooperatively, we hold much power and are getting much done together. That's what an ecosystem does.

Confession. Early on my journey to vibrational awareness, if I was emotionally heavy, I found myself desiring to go to my local Target store. It wasn't because I needed a new random thing, but because I needed all of the genuine kindness I could get from strangers, and the attentive, kind people who worked there fit the bill, so sweetly. I felt welcomed, almost like a special guest, at my local Target. When I had a question or needed help, someone was there. That helping, hospitable nature was the high vibe I needed. These small, mundane exchanges were so refreshing. I wasn't made to feel like I was inconveniencing anyone or disturbing anyone's peace there. I was met with what always felt like a genuine smile and care. And the vibration of kindness and concern in their tone of voice was always very soothing. Almost made me open up and ask for a hug. Okay, moving right along.

But this is what the power of great hospitality and high vibes, no matter the environment, can do. It can transform mundane moments in ways that we may not fully realize someone else may need. We can all be hospitable and radiate helpful vibrations. God knows, the world needs more of this sweet medicine, everywhere.

Becoming a Conduit for High Vibrations

How do we stay dedicated to vibrating higher in a world that's imbalanced? There is a way, and it's to be conduits of nurturing vibrations. We become conduits by using our light, voice, and unique gifts to channel empowering healing energies that counterbalance the ways the world is being misled, wounded, emotionally triggered, torn apart, and underserved. We help the world atone where necessary, mend where necessary, improve where necessary, and eventually be restored to a higher functioning place. And with our awakening, we each can carry out our given supportive role in helping our communities and the greater world vibrate higher—again and again.

Our greatest progress throughout history has been led by awakened people who take on the roles of helper and responder and become conduits for progress and change. All levels of contribution count and matter: we all have different parts to play and different ways to contribute. We can all make a difference in some way. Never underestimate the power of the gifts you carry.

Serve with your
whole heart. As if
you were serving
The Divine.

Offer what
is good for
the soul, not
harmful to it.

After awakening, reconfiguring, and living more deeply into vibrational awareness, you get it. You know firsthand the power (and force) of vibrations, from both ends of life's spectrum, and what they can do. No doubt about it, you've had to overcome some arduous things to gain this (game-changing) insight and power you now hold within you. This is powerful and valuable. And it's vital that you recognize you've been initiated into taking your place in the world as a change agent. You now go into the world with the right amount force and wisdom, because you're fortified to do so.

You know what raises and lowers vibrations, what gives people joy and nourishment, and also what promotes and advances further imbalance and wounds. And as the hero on this path, it's time now for you to become a conduit in the greater world. Look back at what gave you good, healing energy. Then give it to others. Look at what nourishes and empowers you. And in some similar way, transfer that into what it is you do out in the world. For me the strongest vibrations were healthy foods that made me feel nourished and cared for, and friends who loved me—all of me—for who I was. So I try to offer these things to others—through inviting guests to my home to eat a healing meal I prepare with love, and aspiring to be the kind of nurturing friend that I so value and needed on my journey while soul searching.

Vibrational awareness will allow you to stay in tune with what serves people and what harms people. Keep working through your current path, and in spite of any unharmonious forces that may appear, remain kind, compassionate, and decent toward others: keep a pure heart in the world. As a conduit, you're able to contribute to and operate from a separate higher place. And that's the essential part.

Practice being kind and courteous when you usually wouldn't be. Give a compliment when you would typically hold back. Do a good deed for someone. Hold open a door or an elevator for a stranger. Walk, talk, and act with deep integrity. Serve others with your whole heart and mean it. Show up for someone in need. Help others in sadness, aloneness, grief, or distress. Attend to others. Encourage others. Hold space for others. Help others if you have the resources and power to do so. Just be a beautiful vessel out there in the world. Be glorious. Be the hands and ears of The Divine here on Earth.

Tender Zones

A common thing that can happen when you embrace your role as a beacon is that you want everyone to heal, grow, and transform alongside you, and in your time frame. But be easy now: give everyone time and space. This is essential: although you may plant the seeds, everyone grows and learns in their own timing. If you force them, they can grow and unfold prematurely. Remember: we're in a garden. Keep nurturing and planting seeds without forcing others to grow or to flower before their appointed time. Nurture, never force.

Living your life as a beacon is the best teacher, support, and

Many different
beautiful paths
lead to high
vibrations.
Look for the
path awaiting
to take you
higher daily.

Offer your energy, work, and service with integrity, good character, and high intentions in mind.

inspiration for others. Your consistent actions express and penetrate more than your words are able to. As flowers unfolding right in divine time without needing to be forced, the people around you will soak in your nourishing actions like water and light. Their process will be unique like yours was, but it will undoubtedly be helped by your graceful, mindful actions. Start by leading by example, and then once the people around you reach a certain level in their growth process, you can use more grit and inspirational fire with them. They'll have tougher and deeper roots in the ground and will be able to withstand more and more inspirational impact.

Keep in mind that we aren't adopting or taking a problematic mindset of dominance and overcontrol into the world—but one of gracefulness, harmony, and compassion.

Through various collective and cultural pains, as a world, we know where we've been and can now collectively determine to put our energy, efforts, work, and vibration toward the places where we desire to see higher vibrations. It's happening daily. Spirit dance in order here!

So take heart: being a conduit of good energy and a positive influence for others doesn't mean others will transform immediately. The timing of The Divine is never too slow, and we benefit all concerned when we harmonize with this divine timing. This allows us to live in a higher state of peace, awareness, and power even when we aren't in agreement with the path or vibrational state of those around us.

As the alchemy is
happening around you,
just continue being
a beacon and hold
space for growth and
transformation.

Observe. Recognize. Stay in a
state of higher inner power.

Pour from a Full Cup

As conduits of high vibrations and purpose, we must make sure to restore and nurture ourselves along the way. This doesn't mean simply checking in with ourselves from time to time; it means taking time and making space for ourselves in the earliness of our mornings, midday, and again at day's end.

Since nothing is new under the sun, we can rediscover the ancient practice and wisdom of mindfulness as a tool for refilling our cup. Mindfulness is transformative because it calls us to be aware not only of ourselves, but of everything around us. It dissolves the boundary between self and the outside world. It's a tool we can use to deepen, balance, and inform our work as beacons in the world.

We often associate mindfulness with modern times, but the ancient Egyptians, known as the Kemites, had a mindfulness practice that is a beautiful model for us. Each morning the Kemites would set their spiritual and character intentions before heading out into the world. At night they would then reflect on each one of their intentions to gauge how balanced and aligned they remained that day. This practice, still honored and used today by many, is known as the 42 Laws of Ma'at. Ma'at is revered as the ancient Kemetian/Egyptian goddess of justice, harmony, and balance, and the concept of ma'at represents right attitude, balance, and keeping a pure heart. Many faiths have similar practices to keep and support people on the path of right action, balance, fortification, and being pure in heart, while living and interacting in the world. This is a form of vibrational awareness. How are you staying mindful or gauging your own balance, actions, heart, and vibration in the world?

Along the same lines, seeking balance by checking in with ourselves after a day of serving the greater good allows us to examine our cup properly. It's said that you cannot pour from an empty cup. So when serving others, remember to keep your cup full and to be intentional about what you fill your cup with. Stay connected to what positively pours into you, restores you, and helps you to gauge and honor your day-to-day progress. This is daily grace that we can give to ourselves. In the quiet of the morning, set high vibrational intentions for yourself, and as you bring your day to an end, reflect and practice self-examination. And if you didn't hit the day's target, allow grace to step in. The next day is a divine gift to set your intentions and go for it again.

Some of our best ideas and days come from a calm, nourished, and restored mind, body, and soul. We need more of this wholeness and self-care within because it heals, restores, balances, and empowers us to give the same to the world.

How to Pour from a Restored and Full Cup

- Set intentions and regularly check in with yourself.
- Set vibrational boundaries.
- Take stock of everything on your plate and decide what you give your attention to each day, what can wait, and what you can say "no" to.
- Return to what fills and restores you in a nourishing and empowering way.
- Repeat daily.

Implementing mindfulness practices and self-care days in workspaces, at home, and in schools is essential to creating a more balanced, less overstimulated, and less stressed-out world. Self-care is its own conduit, which helps us vibrate higher and feel like ourselves again.

Your Mission and Your Well-Being

We each have our own unique purpose and goals for helping elevate the vibrational state of the world. This process is going to take vibrational work along the way. The work can be hard, but it's our secret weapon in the face of the various tests, triggers, and trials of life.

Take care of yourself as the vessel.

The work needs the proper container—a healthy, nurtured physical body—and it won't start until that is present. Taking good care of yourself is essential to creating the proper container.

Taking care of yourself can include

- Routine wellness checkups
- Physical fitness, dancing, massages, and other ways of discharging accumulated energy from the body
- Slowing down to rest or unwind
- Nourishing meals
- Spending time with supportive people
- Supportive adaptogenic herbs that help you *adapt* to the task at hand
- Spending set apart time doing daily spiritual work

Through trial and error and exploration and discovery, I now know my way. I've found that in order to effectively show up for the daily mission of life, I can't eat anything that gets in the way of my higher potential and well-being. I also have to discharge the accumulated energy I've taken on as a vessel in the world, which I often do through either dance, nourishing baths, or, as of last year, reflexology. Some of the things that keep my vessel healthy and refilled have become part of my daily or weekly routine, while I rotate through others, depending on what my mind, body, spirit, and soul are calling for in order to be supported and renewed. Stay watchful of what your body's calling for.

SACRED WORK

As you continue on the path as a conduit, you will start to see your work as sacred and part of The Divine. Helping others transform, become empowered, and feel more enlightened is a spiritual principle and a way of the mystics and greats throughout time. It's part of the transformation journey of many powerful conduits, past and present, and has been illustrated within the works, lives, and writings of brilliant souls such as Joseph Campbell, Howard Thurman, Inayat Khan, Maya Angelou, Nelson Mandela, Rumi, Martin Luther King Jr., and the Dalai Lama, as we have seen.

In Buddhism, bodhisattvas are individuals who have attained nirvana, but instead of separating themselves from the world or disconnecting from the suffering of others they deliberately choose to remain in the world as beacons and conduits for others. In this way, they help others reach the path of enlightenment. They serve suffering souls from a spiritual place deeply rooted in compassion and higher awareness.

We see this present also in the teachings and life of Yeshua (Jesus Christ), who was both deity and human—beacon, light, and conduit—offering mercy, compassion, hope, grace, and support to the broken and suffering world.

The connection between having high vibrational awareness and using that awareness to help all sentient beings is present in multiple religions. It is not enough that we become awakened, transformed, and free: we must help others as part of our higher purpose and calling. While your path may not specifically model that of Christ or bodhisattvas, you can use their paths as examples for launching into your own life's higher purpose of offering yourself as a light. Reconfiguring and taking your unique gifts, passions, and pains into the world and using them for the greater good is beneficial to all sentient beings. Your work, through a spiritual lens, can look different from everyone else's and still be just as valid, just as spiritual and sacred, and just as necessary, to the world

The Bell

You've most likely at some point reached that universal place where you're wondering whether there's more to life than *this*. And thank

The Divine, our Sender,
forever knows how to
reach us to offer us hope
and a supporting hand
upward into our fuller
selves and higher work.

The Divine, because assuredly there is. And it is beckoning and summoning you forward through your reconfiguration, onward into living your power and your purpose in the world.

I've experienced the call as a bell that rings through vibrations and is present in the innermost depths of my soul. It's always right on time and signals me into action.

Our mission as conduits is to recognize the bell and turn ourselves toward its signaling and purpose. Whether it's the loud bell tower built strong and high within ourselves, or the melodious bells hanging in the peaceful inner temple of our soul, the bell is symbolic of a higher call to action and service. It's a signal of many things. It's a signal to shift in mindset. It's a call to peace or prayer. It's a signal or a call for protection from our Higher Power. It's a mission and assignment into courage and purpose. Through observation and awareness, you'll feel it and you'll know.

When I hear the bell, either I take comfort knowing there is spiritual support and protection in my life, or I know I'm being signaled into a higher duty and action. This call to action or service may be to hold compassion and empathy for someone, to offer a helping hand somewhere, to do or not do a certain thing, or to open up to being a conduit and vessel.

Even before I was aware of the power of vibrations, I knew the power of service. When I spent time in the South with my family as a young girl, I often joined my beloved step-grandmother, endearingly referred to in true black folk Southern fashion as Mama Pug, as she delivered breakfast or dinner plates to the sick, shut in, and homebound. This was how Mama Pug spread love and lived her faith out in the world.

One of my favorite people to visit with her was Ms. Opie, a sweet and frail elderly widow living across the street. I would help Mama Pug clean, straighten up, feed the cat, wash the dishes, and help Ms. Opie get dressed. Sometimes Ms. Opie encouraged me to play dress-up in her glamorous clothes and jewels of old; her beautiful things told sweet stories to my soul, as if they were all alive.

Mama Pug helped other people in the community too. No one went unloved, unfed, or uncared for on her watch. Mama Pug's love created a ripple effect that has impacted my spirit, soul, and consciousness in a mighty way. Those days serving with Mama Pug, when I was a young girl, embedded a love of and seed of caring for others that remains housed within me still, and it's activated today, whenever I hear the bell.

We all hear the bell for different reasons. Maybe a dark night of the soul brought you to discovering your soul mission to serve. Maybe a relationship or an experience inspired a higher shift in your focus and being. Or perhaps the shift is because of the redemption you're seeking for the past. Whatever it is, what called you also made certain you arrived on time—and on cue. This is a universe of mathematical precision and order. You are initiated most often not by choice, but because a divine path has been set before you. When you have risen above, this path transfigures you through the process. So you come out energized, passionate, qualified, and fortified.

As you develop more wholly, becoming capable of functioning at higher potentials and rising above the various vibrations and terrains of life, you, the hero, set out on your own specific path of higher purpose and work in the world. Your path, your influence and expression, can be big or small, seen and unseen.

You've got a new power—a higher vibrational power—now living in and through you and all you do that unquestionably sets you apart from your former self. It's given many names around the world, and all point toward the same thing: reconfiguration, rebirth, nirvana, awakening, transcendence, transformation, and higher purpose.

Removing the Unnecessary Armor

Becoming a teacher for others, healing our surroundings, and gaining some sort of recognition for our wisdom or gifts alone do not make our wellness or our spiritual mission complete. True wellness and higher mission must include the shift into higher aspects of human character, which requires either dismantling or mastering our ego and its many guards and embracing something stronger: kindness.

Living in vibrational awareness and harmony means surrendering to your kinder, high-road-minded self. But don't confuse this with powerlessness. You can still be kind while being assertive and fierce. Think of the Shaolin monks—Buddhist monks in China known for their

What triggers you, controls you.
Have peace, and you control it.

extraordinary fighting skills, self-mastery, and endurance. As monks, they are kind and courteous warrior beings who honor integrity, yet they are also fiercely powerful beyond measure and logic.

Kindness knows when to stand down and when to stand firm, when to put energy and strength out and when to maintain and hold it within. Showing a gentle yet aware character doesn't mean becoming a pushover or being overly vulnerable; it means not allowing your lower vibrations, or the actions of others, to make you an energetic puppet whose strings are pulled any which way. You become poised and the master of yourself and your actions.

Along the same lines, being powerful and being mean are not the same thing. Although it may be a coping or defense mechanism to send out vibrations of meanness, envy, bitterness, apathy, and ill will, this is neither kindness nor power. It's instant gratification and gives a false sense of power.

Where has your character taken you? Where is it steering you?

Embodying the Spiritual Creative

At this stage in your journey, you have widened your lens beyond self-focused growth. Vibrational awareness has taught you that you are not a single, isolated being but are connected to all things. As you grow in this awareness and mature in your role as a giver to the greater good, notice how a higher spirit and power move moves through you and calls you.

On my journey, this higher spirit moved me to tap into my creative energies, particularly through my writing and poetry that offer encouragement and higher intentions. It began as something I did on impulse, as if jolted into action. It was free and out of pure passion and love. I started out cathartically writing for myself, and now I share those writings openly as a conduit to help others.

I had no clue that my writing and work would take on this life of its own and become the full-fledged career path that it has. I simply began where I could, where I felt called, and showed up daily as a vessel and a creative. I had to. The force of the current moving through you has to be channeled into right action—or what you feel won't feel good. It's a living energy that comes through you—as the vessel and conduit—in order to be released out of you. Actualize your gifts. Answer the bell. Whenever I went against this, my vibrations and health suffered. And I'm not alone in this. It is a common occurrence. Doing your thing by living your power is an essential part of how you thrive on all levels.

Spiritual creatives know that their power comes from a higher source, that their gifts are not their own, and that their daily comings, goings, and vibrations are connected to their art forms. They know that they alone cannot, or do not, create the work, but that the work is created through them as an instrument, messenger, and vessel. Spiritual creatives don't create without first seeking and connecting to their Higher Power in a personally sacred way. The creative gift and work are sensed and held sacred. The work environment is held sacred. The work of spiritual creatives is not compromised to feed the ego or to fit into a culture that causes people to lose their power and fall out of higher vibrational alignment. The work is to harmonize and align souls into higher vibrational being. It is The Divine expressing itself through its creation and vessel.

When I think of my favorite spiritual creatives, I quickly think of the vibration-lifting band Earth, Wind & Fire. They see their work as *spiritual work*. Their songs are not only rhythmic and innovative, they're also soulful affirmations of empowerment and higher intentions. One of my favorite songs of theirs, "Spread Your Love," has been a powerful anthem for me as a conduit, among many other songs of theirs. As spiritual creatives, we know that vibrational awareness in our work matters. We have the power to use our gifts to encourage others to rise up and build up. Whatever your calling, mission, gift, or area of service, spread high vibrations through it. The world so needs that.

Inspiration is vital to the spiritual creative, but at times it can come and go in waves. During times of low creative activity, the spiritual creative can turn to things such as self-care, taking time out to play, or rest, time spent in nature, seeking spiritual nourishment, and doing more of what harmonizes the soul. These activities organically reenergize and refresh the creative spirit, drawing inspiration back in—again and again.

Inspiration is what fuels and
ignites the spiritual creative's
work and process. Remaining
connected to a higher source
empowers and sustains it.

A Time of Solace for Spiritual Journeying

On days when the world is overwhelming to live and create in, slow down and breathe deeply in order to calm your mind and nervous system and connect and root into your higher source and place of strength.

We've reached a place where it can appear like we don't need a higher spiritual connection and reverence for it. Maybe it's being neutralized out of our wider culture. But the great thing is that we are prewired for it and can always return home to it, and to its necessary, stabilizing, and empowering current and vibration.

THE
MOVEMENT

As we each tend to the garden of our inner life, we simultaneously act in concert with others doing the same work, and collectively we harmonize toward a higher common good and goal. The marvelous thing about a collective world is that as we each vibrate higher, together we can go farther to serve a greater purpose. I believe we are now experiencing a vibrational awakening, liberation, and movement. We are answering the call for a more fortifying and sustainable way of living so we can grow beyond what we have become. As a species, we must evolve into a higher expression of humankind.

Throughout time, many movements have helped the work progress: the Renaissance, the Scientific Revolution, the Great Awakening, the Abolitionist Movement, the Harlem Renaissance, the Women's Rights Movement, the Civil Rights Movement, the Black Liberation Movement, the Chicano Movement (La Raza), the Environmental Movement, among others. Without these collective movements, we never would have progressed to where we are now.

Similarly, today we are seeing the world differently and no longer accept the status quo as the best we can do. Inequality is not the best we can do. Prejudice is not the best we can do. Institutional racism is not the best we can do. Abusing power is not the best we can do. Low vibrational media, entertainment, culture, and food are not the best we can do.

Old systems and beliefs that have held the world together are disintegrating. In their place is the growing understanding that threads of energy connect all things, and when we harm other people and the environment, all are harmed. The truth has always been present, but now, with vibrational awareness of how everything is interconnected, we're able to fully see and share the awareness.

Are you extending far and wide enough?

Like other great periods of change, we're journeying together toward something better, with questions and increasing concerns for our times. We know that something has to shift and that the tides have to turn. They always turn. Individually and collectively, in small towns and big cities, we're showing up and taking our place to make sure that the tides turn.

Community Showing Up

What does this movement look like? It looks like individual people cooperatively coming together to foster sustainable higher vibrational spaces and provide support to the world.

My bonus grandparents, Mama Pug and Daddy Tom, are bright examples of this support system. They are trustees and elders at their church, the same church that my family and I went to when I was growing up. After my mother died, Mama Pug and Daddy Tom rallied the community church to send bereavement funds to me and my siblings, along with a personal card. Holding the bereavement gift and card, which was written out by the very people I had sung and prayed with as a young girl, I realized I had moved full circle. Mama Pug, Daddy Tom, and the other church elders truly live out songs of love and service in their community. I was touched so deeply by this community experience because it was a reminder of the family and spiritual community that I am still connected to. Both my sister and I were so in need of this kind of supportive, healing,

We must continually outgrow
who we have been, in order to
continually develop into who we
were created to become.

and heart-centered community at that time. Being the steadfast conduit that she is, Mama Pug walked in, with her whole heart.

We all need a safe and snug place to heal and grow so that we can come into our full being. Vibrational-based living helps us see how powerful the right daily routines and environments can be. Social change begins on a community level: be someone who helps create space where others can have a nourishing meal, a sense of safety and community, a heart-healing talk, a laughing good time, a soul hug, or a restorative moment.

We all need a safe place to go where we can soften ourselves. A place we can go when life hurts or is confusing. A place where we don't have to have it all together or know the way forward. A safe place where we can say, "This is my life, help me with it," and "Show me the way." These are the types of intentional spaces that can heal whole communities and that are so vitally necessary.

Take the Community Higher

Deliberate changes in high vibrational community allow people who are living under the influences of lower vibrational environments to have access to what will help set them free and place them on a higher potential path. As a spiritual and wellness guide and educator, I've learned that there are many ways to foster high energies:

- Through moral support, so that spirit and emotional care are priorities and conduits
- Through mindfulness training and stress reduction workshops, so that both mental care and wellness are conduits of balance
- Through healthier food options, so that higher vibrational eating is a conduit for equal thriving, wellness, and healing
- Through more green spaces, so that nature is a conduit
- Through character education, so that self-development and character building are conduits
- Through life-skills training, so that essential and effective life skills for facing events, environments, challenges, and traumas are conduits
- Through high-grade educational curricula, health care, and wellness centers to foster meaningful, whole, and mission-driven lives

Communities that have these resources can safely grow in a higher direction. Be a part of necessary positive change in marginalized and underserved communities and help people there to vibrate higher daily, live their power, and change the game. This community-level vibrational change, just like individual-level vibrational change, is about daily choices. Together, these choices amplify.

Vibrational Literacy

Another strategy for larger change is to increase our vibrational literacy, which means understanding how things have productive and destructive effects. The type of things we support in life matter— businesses, schools, communities, products, creative offerings, and the overall economy. Years ago in downtown Los Angeles's iconic Chinatown neighborhood, Walmart planned to open a new superstore. Let's just say the community wasn't having it. At all. People rallied together and made a fuss, and eventually won. No Walmart in downtown LA. Walmart instead had to come up with a Plan B that would not displace so many local merchants, so the company built a smaller, quainter store called Walmart Neighborhood Market on the outskirts of downtown.

Imagine, if you will, this same type of collective power and mass energy being applied to blocking unhealthy food chains in our inner-city communities. Or toward demanding a vibrational shift of higher standards in the educational system, the media, or the entertainment industry. Collective power and action for good matter and work. So choose what you support wisely, and share vibrational literacy so those in your community can live in their inherent power.

Environmental Wellness

This current vibrational movement toward a greater awareness, which acknowledges that we are part of something happening that is much larger than ourselves, is incomplete without acknowledging the state of the environment and the earth. Vibrational-based living opens our eyes to the wider web of all creation. We learn through this lens that we are but one piece of it, and both we and the web are dependent on each other.

Honoring and revering the earth as our home is a must in order to sustain larger vibrational change. We are divinely appointed caretakers of this world, so it's important to consider the vibrational impact we make and leave behind. We must ask ourselves, Will we uphold our watch and role in raising the collective vibration of this world and time we live in? The need is real. Every day, humankind is desecrating the earth: placing toxins in the air and water; depleting the soil of nutrients; polluting the oceans; emitting greenhouse gases, which destroy the ozone layer; and threatening species and populations of all sorts struggling to survive our modern times. Nature is crying out, and it's counting on us to do better, to vibrate higher, to live in awareness, and to be good, better, stewards and fellow inhabitants of this earth.

The world and environment we live in make deep impressions on us all. We are a product of our environment. Every day we journey through invisible fields of energies that connect us to the earth, one another, the cosmos, and beyond. Remembering this interconnect-

207

Just because a thing

- entertains you
- tastes good to you
- feels good to you
- invites you in
- looks good to you

doesn't mean it's good for you.
Walk in higher discernment,
and live your power.

edness is key to healing the earth. When we help the earth, we help ourselves and others. By helping to raise our own vibration, we contribute harmony and balance to this shared and unified field. We must be and remain ecosystem-minded.

This could look like having greater reverence for nature, and all of the world. It could look like taking only what we need from the environment, living in greater harmony with it and being protectors of it, as many indigenous cultures have done and teach. It can also look like making a mindful effort not to litter or by supporting environmentally friendly companies and brands. What we collectively support sends out a powerful message.

ONWARD: CHANGE THE GAME

Vibrating higher daily is a lifelong practice—both private and collective. Once you have become in tune with what feeds you and what drains you, you become empowered to choose what impacts your daily life. As we collectively gain this awareness and mindset, social change becomes possible. We can change the game.

Power used for vibrational control has been the cause of many problems in the world. *More*, *bigger*, and *faster* are not always better. And they are not always in alignment with the earth's natural rhythms or with the good vibrations that comfort and nurture us. Corrupted power disrupts the flow of high vibrations.

The answer to correcting a history of abuse of power is for us each to live our higher power, one that honors the earth and its offspring.

Each day you receive an invitation to vibrate higher. It all starts within. The most profound and necessary work begins within each of us. The best use and management of our power will always lead toward the higher road and higher vibrations of all concerned. We must ask ourselves:

- How are we each governing ourselves and our vibration?
- How are we each applying the energy and forces of power, dominance, influence, and control in our day-to-day lives and toward others?
- How and where are we each applying the forces of peace, higher intentions, unity, humanity, love, and harmony in our day-to-day lives?

REFLECTIONS

- How do you become aware of the vibrational harm being done to the earth, to ourselves, and to others? In what areas can you become more educated and cultured?
- What parts of your community nurture and foster love, support, and higher vibrational power? How can you get involved?
- What gifts do you offer your community or another community?
- In other words, how will you live your power in service to the world around you? How will you vibrate higher daily and live your power?

Revolutionaries and heroes never left it up
to the system to fix or create the solution.
They became the solution.

To all of the things
that help set us free
to vibrate higher daily,
thank you.

A LETTER
OF LOVE:
EPILOGUE

Dearest One reading this,

I would like to close with a soul letter for the journey ahead. Like a remote outpost in the desert, it stands as an isolated and fortifying area of support for your journey. It's here to lighten the rough times that can spring up (like weeds in a garden) along the way and remind you that I am here—in it and through it all with you.

Full embodiment of vibrational-based living makes all the difference. This is where you go from doing it, to *being* it. I invite you to make it a daily practice instead of keeping it as a separate or occasional part of yourself and your life. When you do this, vibrational awareness becomes all-encompassing in your life and on your unique path, in both the good times and the not-so-good times.

After a while a point will come where it doesn't matter what's going on around you (terrains, weather, or other circumstances) because you are anchored in higher and prevailing awareness that increases your ability to vibrate higher daily and live your power.

Wherever you start each day, whatever spiritual goals you attain, whatever outer visions you dream up and desire to foster and bring about, whatever personal progress or change you desire to see through, and whatever vibrational life you aim to sustain, this book is here to journey with you as a companion. I offer you these closing reminders to keep with you on your path.

Keep a healthy, problem-solving mindset on the journey ahead of you. Troubleshoot when and where necessary to identify problems; to seek positive energy, people, and intentions; and to know what you need to steer away from, move on from, or let go of. Create a path of action.

Keep a journal or create a document that takes note of what's healing you currently and what's causing disharmony. What are any current pain points or blockages? What is helping you fortify and thrive? Stay mindful of different vibrational causes and effects. Communicate with your journal often.

Know when to go alone and when to call in reinforcements. Your reinforcers could be people, practices, or items that offer you support, protection, and/or accountability.

Remember to breathe. On days when stress, illness, or particular problems absorb you and you're not feeling like yourself, breathe deeply and take all the time you need to feel like your empowered self again.

When you feel powerless, remember that the terrains and

weather are challenging you out of your comfort zone and into your higher potential and purpose.

Tend to your wear and tear along the way, as all great journeys produce them. Take time and slow down when necessary.

Even when your role as a conduit gets difficult, remember there is always room for you. You are vital to furthering higher vibrations in the world.

Come back to the pages of this book as needed, and make them a space where you can exhale in grace and maintain your course. May this book, like a form of gravity, keep you from spiraling too far away from yourself and from your post: your goals, mission, purpose, and higher intentions. Stay with, or come back to, a chapter, a section, a reflection, or a practice that you need more time with. There is no rush. When you surrender to divine timing and to the necessary process, you'll realize that you're in good hands—the right hands.

Seek to journey in awareness, grace, and power each day, as you fervently grow and unfold even more into yourself and your purpose. Continue the divine course and purpose set before you.

Now, let some of the best times of your life begin!

From my whole heart,
Lalah Delia
Los Angeles, California
Planet Earth (a.k.a. Earth School)

ACKNOWLEDGMENTS

To The Divine, to my rock, my fortress, you've been so good to me. Couldn't tell it all if I tried. Thank you for loving me. Thank you for knowing me and my past, and for using me still. Thank you for empowering me, for keeping me, and for carrying me through. Thank you for always being there with your sacred power, love, guidance, and medicine. I'm absorbed in it.

Also, thanks for the way you show up in the things and people you've created.

Love and gratitude to my guardian angels for keeping me encompassed.

Mother, thank you for all you've done to deposit into the heart and soul of your children, Michael, Aisha, Matthew, and me: love, kindness, integrity, service, compassion, and seeking daily to have a right and pure heart. I've matured into a deep appreciation for these traits. And I'll always take them with me. Thank you for reading my work and sharing it on your social media. That will always warm my heart. Like you switching your Twitter background, for what would be the last time, to one of my poems, just days before The Divine called you home.

Mother, thanks for showing me what healing, forgiveness, grace, and unconditional love feel like. Case in point, the time when I came clean and confessed to you all of the "skeletons and sins" from when I was lost and running the streets. Right away, you felt it was your fault I had done these things. I told you it wasn't. You began to cry, which I was heavy about yet prepared for. But then moments later, instead of judging, condemning, or disowning me, which I was braced for, you stopped crying, looked up, and you both leaned in closer and asked questions with the most supporting, yet alarming, intrigue. I wasn't prepared for that level of plot twist, Mother. But truly grateful for it. Glad my confession was able to entertain you so much! Totally beats out getting disowned. Thank you for being here on my path of vibrating higher daily. Because of you, I was able to stand in my truth, tell my story, and not be ashamed anymore. Thank you for reminding me of The Divine's amazing grace.

Father, thanks for proving that fathers of color are superheroes too. Thank you for exposing me to what would nourish my mind and soul, like sending me to charm school, exposing me to the arts, and playing soul records growing up. Thanks for being so compassionately patient with my growth into the woman I am ever becoming. Thank you for the frequent two-hour phone conversations about whatever philosophical things are on our mind, and the two-hour phone conversations about nothing much at all. Thank you for always making space for me and for always being a stable source of love in my life. You've been a friend of mine. A really beautiful friend.

To the brave souls who have opened the way, left a trail and a light on. So much gratitude for you, your work, and for the conduits and inspiration that you all are.

Grandmothers, thank you for having a praying spirit. And thank you for teaching me to have one too.

Thank you to my daughter, India, who would see me working tirelessly, and what seemed like without pause on certain days, to complete this book on time, and go into the kitchen "medicine cabinet" and return to my side with an herbal tonic to help me press through.

Thank you to my beloved young Ahsiah, who during the making of this book would call me the sweetest endearing names to make me laugh whenever he saw I needed to take a break and rest, laugh, or play with him. Thank you for being my balance reinforcer.

I'm grateful for all of the ways you two looked after my soul and well-being during the making of this book. Thank you for being such powerful and aligned conduits. And thank you both for sharing me with the writing process. Bless your hearts, real good!

Aisha, the ways you have unconditionally loved me, been there for me, and shown up for me as a sister are beyond expression. Your grace, tenderness, heart, compassion, and laughter are spiritual. Many thanks for your up-close support of my work, journey, well-being, and the writing of this book.

Matthew, your spirit is a divine force. Thank you for holding such sacred space for us all as you officiated our mother's homegoing. That divine service, your grace, poise, words, strength, and peace, which surpassed all understanding, have stayed with me over this past year.

Michael, thank you for basically being Nikola Tesla reincarnated. Seriously! Okay, seriously, I've admired your genius since I was a young girl. I appreciate and hold our recent conversations on vibration, energy, frequency, fasting, and spirituality close to my heart. The fact that I know I can geek out with you is sweet!

Asiya and Devine, you embody the definition of best friend. Thank you both for your huge supporting role in my life.

Laura Lee Mattingly, my heaven-sent literary agent and one

of my biggest supporters throughout. Thank you for helping me breathe outside of the hospital as my mother was fighting for her life. And thank you for rescheduling our meetings with publishers in NYC and California that very same first week of June, as she was then letting go of her fight. Thank you for being there. After canceling the trip and meetings, I had to surrender and put whether or not I would still obtain a book deal in The Divine's hands, and look! Here I am thanking you, and The Divine, for this book being so!

Thank you to the various publishers who so thoughtfully sent cards, books, and warm words of condolence to help comfort me through that time.

Thank you to my publishing family, HarperOne, for still being there when I was able to hold my heart together enough to do this, to begin the process of writing this book. Thanks for believing in me that much, team!

To my editor, Anna Paustenbach, you have been another heaven-sent in my life. I could not have asked for a more aligned and harmonious editor and experience. You've been a huge reason my writing process was such a cathartic one. Thank you for allowing me to pour my heart and soul into this book. I've grown so much with you by my side! I have your initial postcard here on my desk in a special frame. Also, anyone who sends me the book *The Alchemist* is a friend for life.

I'm so beyond grateful, Anna, for the ways vibrational awareness is now integrated into your day-to-day life! You also, Laura Lee! Thank you both for sharing how much working on the book has inspired you both to live it out. This book has changed us all! Group high fives!

HarperOne, thank you for embracing me into the family and for being excited about this book with me. Many thanks to the *Vibrate Higher Daily* team: again, my super-amazing editor, Anna Paustenbach; my production editor, Lisa Zuniga; my creative director, Adrian Morgan; and my publisher, Judith Curr, for giving this book and me a chance to speak to the world And thank you to Mickey Maudlin and Aidan Mahoney for joining the *Vibrate Higher Daily* editorial team.

Thank you all for the love, energy, and support that went into birthing this book into the world. It takes a village! I'm so grateful for your amazing talents!

My cover designer, Megan Mcphill, thank you for being with me before and during the process. Your emails will forever be some of my heart's favorites to open and read. Thanks for the beautiful creative energy that you are and bring.

To my good sister-friends, strong warrior women, all full of grace and purpose, thank you all. Thank you for being the warm and nurturing presence that you all are and for always being within reach. Rachel, sweet sister-in-law, our bond is spiritual soul medicine to me.

Christopher Erskin and my good brother friends, thank you each for your support and soulful friendship.

So many thanks to the teams at Girlboss, Black Girl in Om, MindBodyGreen, and Goop for your support of my work and for offering me space to share my message and work.

To nature, which on many days was my writing office, sanctuary, and sweet place of refuge, quietude, and restoration.

To all of the people, place, and things that inspired me to vibrate higher daily.

I give thanks for the following diverse list of music artists for always helping my mind and spirit release, charge, and feel what it needs to through their music: Earth, Wind & Fire; Lonnie Liston Smith; Sweet Honey in the Rock; Bernice Johnson Reagon; Bob Marley; my sister Aisha Mars; Stevie Wonder; B.T. Express; John Coltrane; Diana Ross; Lecrae; The Clark Sisters; Mahalia Jackson; Marvin Sapp; Mississippi Mass Choir; Bishop G.E. Patterson; William McDowell; Johnathan McReynolds; Sting; Quincy Jones; Thievery Corporation; Sounds of Blackness; Fertile Ground; Mozart; Roy Hargrove; Frankie Beverly; Maze, Brainstorm; Duke Ellington; Chopin; Luther Vandross; Steven Price; Hans Zimmer; Steven

Halpern; Bill Withers; Paul Hardcastle; Sade; Anita Baker; Oleta Adams; Bobbi Humphrey; Shirley Horn; Cesaria Evora; James Taylor; Wendy Waldman; Chavela Vargas; Cheikh Lo; Laraaji; Estas Tonne; Wendy Waldman; RY X; Deuter; Shastro; Caron Wheeler; Michael Franks; Alexandre Desplat; Dario Marianelli; Massive Attack; Zero 7; Guru; *The Wiz* Motion Picture Soundtrack; *The Color Purple* Motion Picture Soundtrack; *Samsara* Motion Picture Soundtrack; and the various artists on my "Energy Cleanse" playlist on Spotify.

To all of my beloved huge family line: the Moores, the Abeytas, the Zamoras, the Beans, the Marshalls, and the Blackmons. Thank you for giving me a rich experience of family, village, and love. A huge gratitude hug to my forever bonus father and siblings, Hardy and the bunch.

To my beloved teachers, mentors, healers, and guides along the way, thank you for taking time with me.

To my younger self, for no matter how hard it was, she did what needed to be done.

And to all of the people who have ever held or carried my purse, phone, baggage, or heart, so I could live freer and fuller in the moment. You matter.

To my readers and supporters, the home crowd, I love you all so much! Thank you for being such a beautiful community to serve. You all have been essential in my process, in this process. Thank you for encouraging me to write a book. Your love and support mean the world to me. I'm rooting for you and cherishing you unceasingly!

And a soul full of gratitude for my grandmothers. Thank you for having a praying spirit. And thank you for teaching me how to have one too. Mama Pug, and your nurturing heart, I'm eternally grateful. Grandmother Lalah and Grandmother Delia, your prayers are still protecting me. It's an honor to carry the names of both of you beloved and spiritually fascinating women. I am divinely blessed.